Dream Symbols and Interpretation

Unlocking the Power of Your Dreams through Symbolism, Mysticism, and Divination for Beginners

© Copyright 2023 - All rights reserved.

The content contained within this book may not be reproduced, duplicated, or transmitted without direct written permission from the author or the publisher.

Under no circumstances will any blame or legal responsibility be held against the publisher or author for any damages, reparation, or monetary loss due to the information contained within this book, either directly or indirectly.

Legal Notice:

This book is copyright-protected. It is only for personal use. You cannot amend, distribute, sell, use, quote, or paraphrase any part of the content within this book without the consent of the author or publisher.

Disclaimer Notice:

Please note the information contained within this document is for educational and entertainment purposes only. All effort has been executed to present accurate, up-to-date, reliable, and complete information. No warranties of any kind are declared or implied. Readers acknowledge that the author is not engaging in the rendering of legal, financial, medical, or professional advice. The content within this book has been derived from various sources. Please consult a licensed professional before attempting any techniques outlined in this book.

By reading this document, the reader agrees that under no circumstances is the author responsible for any losses, direct or indirect, that are incurred as a result of the use of the information contained within this document, including, but not limited to, errors, omissions, or inaccuracies.

Free Bonus from Silvia Hill available for limited time

Hi Spirituality Lovers!

My name is Silvia Hill, and first off, I want to THANK YOU for reading my book.

Now you have a chance to join my exclusive spirituality email list so you can get the ebooks below for free as well as the potential to get more spirituality ebooks for free! Simply click the link below to join.

P.S. Remember that it's 100% free to join the list.

<del>$27</del> FREE BONUSES

- 9 Types of Spirit Guides and How to Connect to Them
- How to Develop Your Intuition: 7 Secrets for Psychic Development and Tarot Reading
- Tarot Reading Secrets for Love, Career, and General Messages

Access your free bonuses here
https://livetolearn.lpages.co/dream-symbols-and-interpretation-paperback/

Table of Contents

INTRODUCTION 1
CHAPTER 1: THE PROCESS OF DREAMING 3
CHAPTER 2: TYPES OF DREAMS 13
CHAPTER 3: THE SYMBOLIC LANGUAGE OF DREAMS 23
CHAPTER 4: DECODING COMMON DREAMSCAPES 39
CHAPTER 5: DREAM THEMES AND THEIR SYMBOLISM 48
CHAPTER 6: DREAM INTERPRETATION METHODS 58
CHAPTER 7: HOW TO DREAM RECALL 69
CHAPTER 8: IDENTIFYING PATTERNS IN DREAMS 79
CHAPTER 9: LUCID DREAMING TECHNIQUES 89
CHAPTER 10: ONEIROMANCY: DREAM DIVINATION 99
CONCLUSION 108
HERE'S ANOTHER BOOK BY SILVIA HILL THAT YOU MIGHT LIKE 110
FREE BONUS FROM SILVIA HILL AVAILABLE FOR LIMITED TIME 111
REFERENCES 112

Introduction

Why do people dream? What do dreams mean? These two universal questions have been on people's minds since ancient times. Throughout history, dreams have been viewed as mysterious occurrences, and there has been no shortage of their possible interpretations. From being harbingers of future events to resolutions of issues to the work of evil forces and deities, dream experiences have been put into numerous contexts across different cultures and belief systems. With the rise of psychoanalysis in the 20th century, scientists started to look deeper into the possible role of dreams in people's lives. This book provides insight into the theories at the forefront of this field, the potential role of dream experiences, and their symbolism as seen through different perspectives.

If you're keen to learn how to give meaning to your dreams, you'll be happy to learn that this book has plenty of practical tools designed for this purpose. It will teach you the universal language of dreams, but this is just the beginning. Did you know that there are common landscapes in many people's dreams? By helping you familiarize yourself with these, the book will empower you with insights into your own dream framework. Equipped with practical tools to decipher common dream themes, you'll be one step closer to interpreting the personal meanings of your dream experiences. These will give you more valuable insight into your dreams and why you have them.

Moving onto a more practical plain, you'll find a chapter dedicated to popular dream interpretation methods, including Jungian dream analysis, Freud's psychoanalytic approach, cognitive dream interpretation, intuitive and reflective approaches, and practical tips and techniques for doing them yourself. Of course, learning how to analyze your dreams wouldn't be too useful if you couldn't recall them, which is a valid concern given that most dreaming happens during **REM** sleep (a deep sleep phase hard to awaken from). Fear not. There is a chapter to explain how to improve your ability to remember and recall your dreams.

It is recommended to keep common symbols and their various meanings in mind, as well as their context and personal significance, and you'll be given hands-on techniques to interpret dream patterns. This will be followed by an explanation of lucid dreams and their interpretation methods. Finally, you'll get to the most intriguing part of the book: the ancient art of oneiromancy, also known as dream divination. From examples shown in ancient literature to how sacred dreams are used across different cultures, you'll explore unique methods to use dreams as spiritual communication. If you're ready to embark on the incredibly empowering journey of unlocking your dreams through their symbolism and spiritual practices, please read on.

Chapter 1: The Process of Dreaming

A dream is a series of involuntary thoughts, images, sensations, and feelings a person experiences while asleep. The process of dreaming takes place during different stages of sleep, although, as you'll learn from this chapter, most dream images are conjured up during REM sleep. Reading it, you'll explore dreams from the initial stages of sleep to the intricate phases of dream formation and delve into the mechanics and sleep cycles, along with the physiological, psychological, and spiritual aspects of dreaming. You'll also learn about the role of REM sleep in dream generation and the brain activity patterns associated with dreams.

The Mechanics of Sleep and Dream Formation

People spend almost a third of their lives asleep.
https://unsplash.com/photos/CwIU33KGToc?utm_source=unsplash&utm_medium=referral&utm_content=creditShareLink

People spend about a third of their lives asleep, making it a crucial part of human well-being. Getting quality sleep is needed for health and happiness because it enables you to build and regulate the pathways in your brain involved in learning and memory formation. Good sleep fosters better focus and response time and is responsible for maintaining several functions of the nervous system, from how your nerve cells communicate and transfer signals between them to how you react to pain and other intense stimuli. One of the main reasons behind this is that your brain never stops working, not even when you're asleep. In fact, sleep is one of the most active phases of the brain, and it's when the removal of negative influences, working through challenging situations, and processing of every stimulus you receive throughout the day happens.

Sleep affects tissues and organs in your body beyond the nervous system. Your quality of sleep affects your heart, lungs, metabolism, and immune system (including the gut, skin, thymus, bone marrow, and spleen). Chronic lack of sleep or inadequate sleep raises the risk of diabetes, high blood pressure, cardiovascular disease, and mental health conditions. Dreams play a critical part in helping your brain fulfill all the roles it needs to perform while you sleep.

Several parts of the brain are involved in sleep and dream formation. These are the most prominent ones:

- **The Hypothalamus**, a structure embedded deep inside the brain, consists of neurons that control sleep and dream formation. Within the hypothalamus is the suprachiasmatic nucleus (SCN), represented by a large cluster of neurons that communicate directly with your eyes. When your eyes are exposed to light, they signal to the SCN that you should be awake and signal to the brain that it must function accordingly. When you're in the dark, your eyes signal to the SCN that you should be asleep, and the brain can start dream formation. People with damaged eyes or SCN will sleep erratically throughout the day because they can't match their circadian rhythms with the natural light-dark cycle. Consequently, their dream formation will be affected, too.

- **The Thalamus** acts as a messenger between the cerebral cortex (the superficial layer interpreting and converting information from short-to long-term memory) and other parts of the brain.

During most stages of sleep, the thalamus is inactive, letting your brain tune out external stimuli and contributing to successful dream initiation. During REM sleep, however, the thalamus gets activated and sends the cerebral cortex sensations, sounds, images, and ideas you'll experience in your dreams.

- **The Brain Stem** is a structure at the very base of the brain. It affects the hypothalamus and its ability to make the transition between wakefulness and sleep. Both the hypothalamus and the brain stem release the neurochemical GABA, which dials back the activity of arousal centers in the hypothalamus and the brain stem. The brain stem also has a key role in REM sleep. At this stage, it conveys signals to relax the muscles essential for limb movements and posture, preventing you from physically acting out your dreams.

- **The Basal Forebrain** is located at the bottom part of the front brain lobe. Like the hypothalamus, it also controls sleep and wakefulness. Its cells release adenosine, a chemical that encourages better sleep and adequate dream formation.

- **The Pineal Gland**, situated within the two brain hemispheres, is in contact with the SCN. After receiving adequate signals of a lack of light, the pineal gland starts producing the sleep-promoting hormone melatonin, which makes it easier to fall asleep after dark. Melatonin is released in different amounts over time, matching the body's circadian rhythm to the cycle of light and darkness.

- **The Amygdala** is a tiny nut-sized structure that is responsible for processing emotions and is found to become highly active during REM sleep. It's another structure linked to active dream formation.

Sleep Stages and Mechanisms

Sleep Stages and Their Role in Dream Formation

Experts distinguish two basic forms of sleep, which are REM and non-REM sleep. The latter is further broken down into three stages, each associated with specific brain patterns and neuron activity. You go through several cycles of all of the non-REM and REM sleep stages during a good night's sleep, although REM sleep becomes longer toward the second half of the sleep. Most of the dreaming occurs during REM sleep, and the more REM sleep you get toward the morning, the more likely it is that you'll remember your dreams.

The first stage of non-REM sleep is when your brain shifts from its conscious wakeful state to sleep. It only lasts a few minutes and is characterized by light sleep. Your brain waves adopt a much slower pattern, which helps your brain slow your breathing, heartbeat, and eye movements. Your muscles relax, although you may experience periodic twitches in your arms and legs.

The second stage of non-REM sleep is a relatively long phase of light sleep you experience before your brain enters a deeper state of unconsciousness. Your breathing and heartbeat slow down even more, your eye movements cease, your muscles relax completely, and your body temperature lowers. This is the consequence of slowed brain activity. However, your brain may still display short bursts of wave activity. This is how your body prepares for dream initiation.

The third stage of non-REM sleep is characterized by a period of profound sleep (the kind that leaves you feeling well-rested). It's more common in the first half of the night and is known for the slowest breathing and heartbeats you experience during sleep. Because your brain waves are even slower, it indicates that the brain has cleared up any obstacles and is now ready to enter the dreaming phase.

The first period of REM sleep follows about an hour and a half after your brain enters the first non-REM stage. This stage got its name after the side-to-side rapid eye movements that occur behind closed eyes. Brain wave activity increases and starts alternating between different wavelengths, similar to what occurs during wakefulness. Likewise, your heartbeat speeds up and becomes irregular. You may be experiencing vivid dreams. However, because they happen during the REM stage (a stage from which it's the hardest to wake up), you will be unlikely to remember your dreams.

Sleep Mechanisms

The circadian rhythm is the main mechanism responsible for regulating sleep and dream formation. Circadian rhythms command numerous bodily functions, from hormonal release and metabolism to body temperature to fluctuations between sleep and wakefulness. They control when you fall asleep, cause you to be sleepy at night, and recognize your natural wake-up time in the morning. The circadian rhythm is governed by your body's biological clock, a system that follows a 24-hour day. Besides light and day, circadian rhythms also rely on other environmental cues (like temperature) to determine what time of the day it is, but for a short time, they can work on their own. With a healthy circadian rhythm, you can get enough quality sleep and form dreams while asleep. Conversely, if your circadian rhythm is altered, you'll have trouble falling asleep and sleeping through the night, and your brain won't be able to form dreams either.

The Role of REM Sleep in Dream Generation

The brain is more active during the dreams of REM sleep than at any other time except wakefulness, allowing the brain to continue to function at a high level. This enables the brain to form dreams made of images, thoughts, sensations, and other stimuli.

Thanks to the advances in neuroimaging and technology and the scientists' keen interest in sleep health and dreaming, there has been a lot of research about the role of REM sleep during dream formation. When you're asleep, your mind is in an unconscious state, which makes it harder for it to process memories. However, dreams during REM sleep enable the brain to recall memories from your waking life, relive them, and process them, along with the emotions they generate. Studies suggest that REM sleep's role extends beyond letting the brain relive past experiences (Hobson et al., 2014; Kirov, 2013) to generate more efficient resolutions to issues after awakening. Besides alluding to the ability of dreams to consolidate emotionally loaded memories, this also indicates that dream experiences represent a real-world simulation of problem-solving techniques the brain generates based on emotional coping strategies (Revonsuo et al. 2015).

The Brain Activity Patterns Associated with Dreams

The role of the unconscious mind in the whole process of dreams can also be measured by the different brain activity patterns associated with dreams. Studies involving EEG (Electrooculography) waves confirm the presence or absence of dreams during different sleep stages (Marzano et al., 2011). The same types of brain waves that occur in the waking state were found during sleep, which suggests a time frame that the brain spent on reprocessing events from the wakeful state. The strongest of these brain waves are called theta waves. Their activity is linked to memory formation in waking life, like when you learn new information and can easily recall it afterward. Their increased activity during sleep (particularly during REM sleep) suggests that dream experiences represent complex emotional and thought processes your brain manages day and night.

The Purpose and Function of Dreams

The purpose of dreams has intrigued people for centuries. The famous Greek philosopher Aristotle claimed that dreams are the consequences of residual movements made by major sensory organs. On the other hand, psychiatrist Sigmund Freud affirmed that dreams were nothing but metaphors for repressed inner needs. While the discovery of REM sleep and its function disproved many of these early theories, continued research has discovered new information about the purpose and function of dreams. Below are the most well-known theories about dreaming.

The AIM Theory

The AIM Theory of Dreaming (Activation Synthesis Theory) was devised by J. Allan Hobson in 1978. According to this theory, dreams stem from neurobiological aspects, like basic survival and reproductive needs. Because they are needed for survival, these functions remain active during sleep. The theory claims that dreams aren't psychologically driven but an effort of the brain to create an alternative narrative for essential neurobiological functions so it can keep you alive.

The Threat Simulation Theory

Similar to the previous theory, the Threat Simulation Theory (developed by Antti Revonsuo) argues that dreams are solely an evolutionary means to an end and are essential for survival. According to this theory, your brain rehearses actions you can take in potentially dangerous situations, enabling you to brain-prepare adequate action for threatening events you may experience during wakefulness. This idea is based on the fact that fear and anger are the most common feelings people remember from their dreams. It further indicates that dreams also have an adaptive role, although this has been disputed nowadays because modern society has far fewer dangers than primitive human societies did. That said, even if survival isn't frequently at risk, your dream still wants to prepare for the event when it may happen.

The Contemporary Dreaming Theory

The Contemporary Theory was devised by Ernest Hartmann, who claimed that the brain must establish connections between abstract concepts and simple thoughts (the link representing the basis of healthy mental functions). While these connections form actively during the wakeful state, they will be present during sleep too, only they'll be looser, leading to dream formation (Hartmann, E. 1996). According to this theory, dreams are actively shaped by the feelings accompanying the thoughts populating your brain while asleep. Underlining this idea, research showed that dream experiences are often more focused, and people have more intense dreams after traumatic events (Hartmann, E. 2010).

The Expectation Fulfillment Theory

This theory suggests that dreaming enables you to work through sentiments you find difficult to adequately express while you're awake. Based on this, dreams are metaphors that represent feelings you feel appropriate to act on during wakefulness or don't feel safe to express outside of sleep. Processing these elements during sleep helps you to function properly the next day. This is underlined at an early age by the characteristics of **REM** sleep during dream development when survival instincts are etched into people's brains. Because dreams don't require a simulation of your waking life, they don't affect sensory and motor activity, only your memory. This process nurtures the unusually creative narratives, thought patterns, and imagery your mind conjures up in your dreams.

The Night Therapy Theory

This theory was formulated by Matthew Walker, who believes that sleep is essential not just for healing physical conditions and injuries but for healing emotional wounds, too. Noradrenaline, the hormone released in response to anxiety, can't affect the brain in **REM** sleep. At the same time, many brain centers of emotional processing and memory recall are activated. This allows the brain to work through feelings and unpleasant memories in a stress-free environment. The latter discovery led to the belief that preventing a person from reacting to emotions without properly processing them could be one of the primary roles of dreams.

The Role of Dreams

Conflicting theories about the functions of dreams notwithstanding, dreams have plenty of proven benefits, including, but not limited to, the ones listed below.

They're Therapeutic

Your dreams could be your mind's way of confronting emotional issues and traumas you've experienced in your life. Remember, your brain is operating at a much more emotional level in your sleep, so your unconscious mind can make connections between your feelings, and your conscious mind can't. Because REM-sleep dreaming lacks the drive to act out dreams, it's easier for you to process traumatic, emotional events, offering sound resolution after awakening.

They Enhance Fight-or-Flight Training

The amygdala, which is a tiny brain structure partially responsible for the fight-or-flight response and the survival instinct, is more engaged during dreaming (especially during REM sleep). Similarly to how the amygdala promotes you to react to potentially dangerous situations in waking life, it's preparing the brain for threats in your sleep. Fortunately, the muscle relaxing signals sent out by the brain stem prevent you from moving. However, the threat you perceive during your dreams could indicate that you feel threatened in real life as well, only for a different reason.

They Boost Critical Thinking

Non-REM empowers memory retention, while REM sleep connects the stored memories and blends them in a unique way. While dreaming, your brain works hard through a vast array of acquired knowledge, draws conclusions, and creates a mindset that can help you find solutions to challenging problems.

This was confirmed by a study (Walker et al. 2002), which tested this by waking up participants from several stages of sleep during the night. Participants were awakened from REM sleep and non-REM sleep and given short tests to assess their problem-solving skills (like puzzles). For comparison purposes, participants took the same tests beforehand. Then, their brain waves were monitored during their sleep so they could be woken at different points during the night. When roused from the non-REM stage, participants had insufficient creativity to solve more than a few puzzles. In contrast, when woken during REM sleep, they solved up to 35 % more puzzles, which is even more than they did while awake. Moreover, most participants woken at this stage said that they found resolving the issues effortless, almost as if the solution would just appear in front of their mind's eyes.

In a similar study (Walker et al. 2007), participants were introduced to a series of relational facts, and their understanding was tested through a series of questions. The participant's performance on this assignment was measured before and after an hour-long nap that included REM sleep and again after a full night's sleep. Those who had adequate sleep (or a long nap) performed much better on this assessment than when they were awake. This study underlies the difference between learning knowledge (otherwise known as the retention of facts) and wisdom (knowing what each fact means individually, how they fit together, and learning their combined meaning). The latter happens in REM sleep dreaming.

They Enhance Creativity

Dreams are thought to enhance creativity.
https://www.pexels.com/photo/woman-in-brown-scoop-neck-long-sleeved-blouse-painting-933255/

You have probably heard of artists claiming the inspiration for their work came to them in their dreams. Perhaps you have woken up with a great idea yourself, only you didn't know where it came from. Dreams lack logic, which often inhibits creativity in waking life. Without logic restricting your thinking process, your creativity soars, and you find solutions for even the most challenging hurdles.

They're Great Memory Aides

Dreams enable your brain to store and catalog critical memories - whether facts you've learned or experiences you created. They also help eliminate inconsequential memories (like facts your brain doesn't find useful) and sort through complicated thoughts and emotions. It's a well-known fact that if you learn new information and go to sleep shortly afterward, you'll be able to recall it better than without sleeping on it. While the way dreams affect memory retention and recall is still uncharted territory, it's generally accepted that dreams enable the brain to learn efficiently. Besides working on storing relevant information even in your sleep, your brain completes this task by blocking out stimuli that could interfere with learning and memory retention.

They Represent an Avenue for Spiritual Connections

Dreams have long been associated with spirituality. Different cultures have used dreamwork to connect to spiritual realms, spirits, and people's own spiritual (higher) selves. As you recall, in sleep, your mind is in a unique state of subconsciousness, which is similar to a trance state, except it's much deeper. Like trances, dreams also enable you to process spirituality-related ideas and feelings on a much deeper level. If you're looking into a spiritual journey or simply exploring your spiritual beliefs, analyzing your dreams can be a wonderful way to start. Moreover, spiritual practices like divination can also benefit from dreamwork and dream analysis, which is why dreams have been part of prophetic practices for thousands of years.

Chapter 2: Types of Dreams

Humans have been captivated by dreams throughout the ages. From ancient civilizations to modern societies, dreams have been considered gateways to other worlds and are sometimes considered a source of divine messages. Dreams have inspired an array of emotions, from awe and wonderment to fear and panic. Individuals often seek a better and deeper understanding of their dreams. This helps them to understand their subconscious self and to bridge the gap between their waking and sleeping lives.

If you dig deeper, you'll realize at the very core of this fascination lies the idea that dreams offer humans a unique glimpse into the workings of the subconscious mind. The kaleidoscope of emotions, experiences, and thoughts you experience when asleep helps you understand yourself better. In this chapter, you'll embark on a journey toward unlocking the secrets of the vivid imagery you experience when you are asleep, untethered by the shackles of waking reality. You'll learn about various types of dreams, explore their significance, and gain insight into their distinct characteristics and emotions. These dreams act as a window to understanding the different and complex aspects of your psyche, and this chapter will equip you with the strategies you need to confront unresolved emotions, find creative inspiration, and gain clarity in your waking life while asleep.

Prophetic Dreams

Prophetic dreams often leave a profound impact on those who experience them. They're characterized as experiencing future events while you're asleep. Sometimes, it's a helpful nudge in the right direction when you're confused, and for others, it's a unique vision offering them insight into a particular decision. While prophetic dreams are extensively synonymous with religious beliefs, you don't necessarily need to identify with a religion to experience one. You could have experienced a prophetic dream but found it challenging to distinguish it.

Merriam-Webster defines prophetic dreams as *"Relating to, or characteristic of a prophet or prophecy"* or *"foretelling events."* A dream offering you a glimpse into the future is characterized as a prophetic dream and is vivid, incredibly detailed, and emotionally significant. Experiencing one will leave a lasting impression on your waking life, and unlike fragmented dreams, you need to piece them together. Prophetic dreams have a coherent storyline that unfolds with clarity, so you understand the message it's trying to convey.

Before moving forward, let's look at the religious symbolism of prophetic dreams. They've played a significant part in shaping the dynamics of faith worldwide and experiencing them, especially if you identify with a religion, as a sign of spirituality. Different faiths have varying beliefs. While some regard prophetic dreams as private conversations between a God and his followers, others believe they are omens foretelling good or bad fortune.

Prophetic Dreams in the Bible

The Bible records many rich instances of prophetic dreams. In Numbers 12:6, God declares that when a prophet is among his people, the Lord reveals himself to them in visions and speaks to them in dreams, bestowing on them messages of profound significance. In the Bible, prophetic dreams can be observed manifesting in various forms. Some act as a beacon of encouragement, guiding individuals toward God in times of uncertainty. For instance, in the book of Matthew, a dream experienced by Joseph recounts his experience when Mary was pregnant. The dream assured him not to fear her pregnancy and to advance with their plans to get married.

Some prophetic dreams come with potent warnings and advise the individual to prepare for challenges. Pharaoh's dream foretold a famine.

The dream urged him to store food and ensure the well-being of his people. Valuable insights from these dreams offer a chance to prevent calamity.

Prophetic dreams can also extend beyond the scope of individual lives and reveal glimpses of the future. Joseph's dream in Matthew 2 called for him to make a decision in response. It asked him to return to Nazareth from Egypt using a different route than the one he had planned to prevent Herod from murdering Jesus. Likewise, Paul's dream in Acts 16 asked him to act immediately and help someone.

Prophetic Dreams in the Quran

According to Islamic teachings, dreams are closely linked to Prophethood and hold a special significance for believers. Prophet Muhammad (peace be upon Him) stated that dreams are one of the forty-six parts of Prophethood. The truthfulness of the dream is closely linked to the sincerity of the dreamer, and those who regularly practice honesty in their speech are more likely to experience truthful dreams.

The followers of the Islamic faith believe that the world as it is known today will end one day, and everyone in this universe, from its beginning to the very end, will be put on trial for their deeds in this life and granted either paradise or hell in the afterlife. As the world progresses closer to the end of times, dreams will become more accurate and meaningful for believers. They can bring good news during tumultuous times or serve as a means of divine communication.

Islam also provides guidelines for its followers to experience true dreams. The faith says that whoever wishes to have true dreams should practice truthfulness in their speech, eat only halal food, and adhere strictly to the commandments laid down by Allah and His Messenger (peace be upon Him). The religion also says that the practicing individual must face Qiblah in a state of purity when asleep and keep remembering their lord until their eyes feel droopy and heavy. An individual practicing this will hardly ever experience untrue dreams.

Distinguishing Prophetic Dreams from Regular Dreams

C.G. Jung, the renowned Swiss psychoanalyst and psychiatrist, looked deeper into the world of predictive dreams and discovered identifying characteristics that distinguish predictive dreams from ordinary ones. According to Jung, the key to identifying a predictive or prophetic dream lies in the intense emotional reaction it triggers within an individual. Throughout your life, you will notice that regular dreams may fleetingly pass through your mind and fade from your memory minutes after you're awake. However, predictive dreams leave a mark that will be etched into your consciousness for a significant time.

Ancient civilizations were aware of this distinction and often classified dreams into two categories. The *"small dreams"* are considered wanderings of the mind and are forgettable, but the *"big dreams"* leave an impact on those who experience them and hold transformative power. The *"big dreams"* impact the dreamer's personality and help to shape their understanding of the world around them.

Jung's exploration of predictive dreams explores the dynamics of connections between dreams and human experience. It dissects the experience of prophetic dreams on individuals and how it opens a gateway to deeper levels of consciousness. The more you explore the landscape of your *"big dreams,"* the more you'll learn to pay attention and understand the secrets that can profoundly shape your life. Their significance isn't limited to offering glimpses into the future, but they also provide the capacity to transform the hidden aspects of your personality.

Lucid Dreams

Unlike typical dreams where the dreamer is unaware of its illusory nature and remains passive, lucid dreaming opens the doorway to a realm where the dreamer is aware and in control of their dream. It's a way to heighten your consciousness, allowing you to recognize that you're in a dream and capable of manipulating it.

In a lucid dream, the dreamer becomes a conscious participant in the dream world. This state of awareness allows them to interact with the dream environment and with dream characters and alter the dream's progression. It is like being both the actor and the director of a surreal and captivating play on the stage of the subconscious. However, you may sometimes experience different levels of consciousness and control when experiencing lucid dreams. At the most basic level, you'll realize that you're dreaming and understand its nature but lack significant control over the dream's unfolding. At the highest levels of lucidity, individuals can influence the dream's narrative, scenery, and even their actions within the dream. The deeper the level of lucidity, the more profound the impact on the dreamer's experience and potential for personal growth.

In a lucid'dream, you're immersed in the dream environment.
https://pixabay.com/photos/fantasy-light-mood-heaven-lovely-2861107/

Benefits of Lucid Dreaming

With its unique ability to grant conscious awareness within the dream realm, lucid dreaming provides you with a treasure trove of benefits extending far beyond the boundaries of ordinary dreaming. As a dreamer steps into this world of lucidity, they unlock transformative possibilities and valuable insights that can enrich their waking lives. Let's look at how you can harness lucid dreaming to better understand yourself and the world around you.

Utilizing Lucid Dreams for Creativity and Problem-Solving

Think of lucid dreaming as your personal playground for creativity. You'll be amazed at the endless possibilities in this wonderland of dreams. Artists can let their creativity flow, writers can pen epic tales, and inventors can brainstorm groundbreaking ideas. There are no limits to what you can achieve within the boundless reaches of your lucid dreamscapes.

Not only is lucid dreaming a realm of endless creativity, but it's also a secret weapon to help you tackle real-life challenges. You'll have the chance to play detective with your own mind, seeking solutions to problems that may have seemed impossible in waking life. As you dive deep into your subconscious, you'll find hidden gems of insight and inspiration waiting to be discovered.

Don't be surprised if you wake up with a lightbulb moment, a brilliant idea that surfaced from the depths of your lucid dreams. Many renowned inventors, writers, and artists have credited their lucid dreams with providing them with breakthroughs and fresh perspectives.

For instance, let's take a journey back in time to explore the fascinating life of Albert Einstein, one of the most renowned scientists in history. His contributions to the field of physics, particularly his groundbreaking theory of relativity, have revolutionized the understanding of the universe. However, a little-known aspect of Einstein's brilliance may surprise you, and that was his relationship with dreams.

Einstein's theory of relativity, which laid the foundation for modern physics, is said to have emerged from the depths of his subconscious mind. While it can't be said with certainty that he was a lucid dreamer, as the term was not officially recognized during his lifetime, it is evident that Einstein made the most of his sleeping life. He understood the value of dreams as a gateway to untapped creativity and insight. Einstein pondered the nature of consciousness and the very fabric of reality throughout his life. He famously questioned whether "reality is a mere illusion," indicating his fascination with the world of dreams and their boundless possibilities. It is believed that he used his dreams to his advantage, exploring complex scientific ideas within his subconscious.

Just think about it. You'll spend about a third of your life asleep, immersed in the mysterious realm of dreams. Could it be that some of the most profound moments of genius and creativity in human history have come from tapping into that otherworldly domain? Einstein's case certainly makes you wonder.

Overcoming Fears and Phobias through Controlled Dream Experiences

Think of a fear or phobia holding you back in your waking life. It could be the fear of heights, the terror of spiders, or the anxiety of public speaking. In lucid dreaming, you can bravely confront these fears, knowing they are products of your mind. With the shield of lucidity, you step into your dream with confidence and determination. The once overwhelming fear loses its grip on you as you explore it from a place of control. You may face the fear directly or transform it into something less intimidating, like a friendly companion or a harmless object.

As you engage with your fears in this empowered state, you begin to build resilience and inner strength. The dream becomes a training ground for your mind, where you rewrite the narrative of your anxieties. Each time you face fear in a lucid dream, you chip away at its power over you in waking life. The beauty of lucid dreaming is that it provides a safe space for exposure therapy. By repeatedly confronting your fears within the dream realm, you desensitize yourself to their impact. As you gain control over these fears in your dreams, you will notice that they also start losing their hold on your waking self.

The experience of conquering your fears in lucid dreams can foster a profound sense of self-empowerment. You carry this newfound courage into your everyday life, transforming how you approach challenges. The insecurities that once held you back lose their sway as you step into the world with newfound bravery.

Cultivating Lucid Dreams

Gaining control over your dreams is a skill that can be mastered with practice. You can use proven techniques to help you unlock the gateway to lucidity, and dreamers have perfected these methods to experience the highest levels of lucid dreaming.

Reality Checks

Reality checks are a simple yet effective way to trigger lucidity within your dreams. Throughout your waking hours, pause for a moment and ask yourself, "Am I dreaming?" Perform a reality check, like trying to push your finger through your palm or looking at a digital clock twice to see if the numbers change. You'll carry the habit into your dreams by practicing these checks frequently. When you perform a reality check within a dream, you may just realize that you are, indeed, dreaming!

Mnemonic Induction of Lucid Dreams (MILD)

MILD is a powerful technique that involves setting strong intentions before falling asleep. As you drift off to dreamland, repeat a phrase like, "I will become lucid in my dreams," with utmost conviction. Visualize yourself, recognizing that you're dreaming, and imagine the excitement of achieving lucidity. This powerful affirmation imprints the idea of lucid dreaming onto your subconscious, increasing the likelihood of becoming lucid during your dreams.

Wake-Back-to-Bed (WBTB) Technique

The WBTB technique involves waking up from your sleep, staying awake for a short while, and then going back to sleep. Set an alarm to wake you up after about five hours of sleep. During this wakeful period, engage in calming activities like reading or jotting down your dream experiences. This enhances your awareness and primes your mind for lucidity when you return to sleep.

Recurring Dreams

You know that feeling when you step into a recurring dream, like you've been there before, living the same scenes repeatedly? Recurring dreams are like a captivating puzzle, filled with patterns and themes that seem to beckon you into their mysterious embrace. In these dreams, you may find yourself in familiar places or facing similar situations repeatedly. It's as if your subconscious is trying to convey something of great importance. The characters and events may vary slightly, but the underlying essence remains consistent.

For instance, you find yourself fleeing from an unknown entity or an unseen force. No matter how fast you run, the chaser persists, leaving you with a deep sense of fear and anxiety, or you may experience falling dreams evoking a stomach-lurching sensation as if you're plummeting into an abyss. Each of these recurring dream themes carries symbolic significance, reflecting areas of your waking life that may need attention or resolution.

The key to deciphering your recurring dreams lies in paying close attention to the details. Journal your dreams diligently, capturing every element, emotion, and interaction. As you review your entries and patterns, consider your dreams' recurring themes and emotions. Are there unresolved conflicts or fears that need to be addressed? Is there a recurring pattern in your relationships or behavior that you need to change? Reflect on your dreams' messages and take steps to resolve underlying issues. Breaking the cycle of repetition may involve making conscious changes in your waking life. Embrace new perspectives, face your fears, and overcome negative patterns. As you bring awareness and transformation to your waking self, your dreams may also evolve, reflecting your journey of self-discovery.

False Awakening Dreams

Have you ever experienced the uncanny feeling of waking up and going about your morning routine, only to realize that it was all an illusion? The intriguing phenomenon of false awakening dreams, where reality and dreams intertwine, has perplexed dreamers forever. In these dreams, you believe you have woken from slumber and are going about your daily activities. The scenes seem so realistic that it's challenging to discern between the dream and waking worlds. It's like being trapped in a series of mirrored reflections, where each awakening leads to yet another illusion.

As you explore false awakening dreams, you'll find different levels of complexity. Sometimes, you may experience a single false awakening while, at other times, you may encounter multiple layers of dreams nested within one another. These dreams can be deceivingly real, leaving you questioning the boundaries between waking and dreaming.

Symbolism in False Awakening Dreams

Nested Dreams

One of the intriguing aspects of false awakening dreams is the presence of nested dreams within each other. Each awakening is like peeling back the layers of an enigmatic dream onion. These dreams can carry profound symbolism, reflecting the many facets of your subconscious mind. Analyzing nested dreams can provide valuable perception into your emotions, fears, and desires. Pay attention to the transitions between the nested dreams, as they reveal unresolved issues or areas of your life that require attention.

Altered Reality

The familiar environment may undergo subtle or significant changes in false awakening dreams. Rooms could shift in size or location, objects may morph into something else, and the people you encounter could take on unexpected roles. The altered reality in false awakening dreams can represent the fluidity of your perceptions and the malleability of your mind. It's a reminder that reality, too, can be subjective, influenced by your thoughts and emotions.

Nightmares

Nightmares emerge from the depths of your subconscious mind, leaving you in a state of terror and unease. These haunting dreams are distinguished by their vividness, intense emotions, and unsettling themes that often linger long after you wake. Within nightmares, your deepest fears and anxieties take center stage. Nightmares profoundly impact your emotional well-being, leaving you with a lingering sense of discomfort and fear, even in the light of day.

Your nightmares may reflect the emotional turmoil you are experiencing, offering an opportunity to confront and process these feelings. They can be seen as the subconscious mind's attempt to bring unresolved issues to the surface, urging you to face them with courage and compassion.

Night Terrors

Night terrors, distinct from nightmares, are characterized by their intense and distressing nature, often leaving individuals in extreme fear and agitation during sleep. Unlike nightmares, which are bad dreams that can be recalled upon waking, night terrors are usually forgotten, leaving individuals confused and disoriented. These episodes typically occur during non-REM sleep and can involve sudden screaming, thrashing, and a sense of terror.

Night terrors are more common in children, but adults can also experience them. Understanding the themes of night terrors is essential to help you unravel their underlying causes, which can be triggered by factors such as sleep deprivation, stress, anxiety, and certain medications.

By delving into the diverse types of dreams and their potential interpretations, you've gained a powerful skill: the ability to classify your dreams. Armed with this knowledge, you can now discern prophetic dreams from lucid dreams, understand recurring dreams, and navigate the haunting mysteries of nightmares and night terrors. Dream analysis has become your invaluable tool for personal growth, providing you with a window into your subconscious mind and guiding you toward self-awareness.

Chapter 3: The Symbolic Language of Dreams

The world of dreams is vast and full of mystery. Nothing is ever as it seems. You can dream of color, number, or animal and think this is just a random image. However, there is a deeper meaning behind everything you see. Understanding it will give you a better insight into your unconscious mind.

This chapter covers the meaning behind different dream symbols so you can easily interpret your dreams.

The Nature of Symbols and Their Role in Dreams

Many people don't pay attention to the images they see in their dreams because they believe these symbols are random and don't make any sense. However, dream symbols can be a type of self-expression. You're creating stories and images that reflect your truest emotions, which you may not be aware of in your waking life. They connect your innermost feelings to your real world to show you things that you might have missed and push you to take the necessary actions.

Symbols are the language of dreams. When you understand what they mean, you'll be able to interpret what your dreams are trying to tell you. Each symbol has a deeper meaning than what you see on the surface. For instance, a dog in your dream is more than just a pet or an animal you love. It can represent friendship and loyalty. However, symbols can also be interpreted based on experiences, beliefs, and cultural backgrounds. If you have had a bad experience with a dog before, it can mean betrayal or that you're going through a hard time. The way the dog behaves is also crucial to interpreting your dream. The meaning behind a calm dog is also different from a dog that is attacking you. So, there are various elements to take into consideration when interpreting a dream.

Your cultural background and beliefs will also influence your dream interpretations. For instance, a cow or a cross can have different meanings in different religious beliefs. Some objects also have a collective meaning, such as a cross representing sacrifices for all Christians.

For centuries, the concept of symbols has meant to connect a person to something that is unfamiliar but valuable to them. So, the symbols you create in your dreams form a connection to all the possibilities you don't even know exist. They convey complex ideas, emotions, and experiences that are beyond yourself in a condensed and metaphorical form.

A metaphor is finding the word or phrase associated with an object that isn't its literal meaning. While symbolism is finding the association between two events or objects. One symbol or metaphor can have different meanings behind them.

The Greek philosopher Aristotle once said that the greatest dream interpreters have the power to observe resemblances (metaphors). He added that the ability to see the metaphors behind dream symbols allows you to connect and interpret their meaning. Ancient Greek dream interpreter and diviner Artemidorus said that dream interpretation is noticing the contrast between similarities.

Interpreting symbols can be complicated. Sometimes, metaphors seem strange. However, if you pay attention to what you say in your daily life, you will notice that you usually use metaphors in conversations like "Life is a highway" or "I am feeling under the weather." This is why you dream in metaphors because your mind is accustomed to making similar associations.

However, some dreams are direct. For instance, a dog can be your family pet, while on some occasions, it can be indirect. If you have never had a dog before or haven't thought of or seen one in a while, this image will seem random to you, so you should investigate the meaning behind it.

You don't just dream about your daily life. Your mind creates symbols that may or may not be familiar to you to open your eyes to significant things in your waking life. On the surface, dream imagery may seem strange, but, in reality, they are metaphors with deeper meanings.

Dreams can open your eyes to significant things in your waking life.
https://pixabay.com/illustrations/fantasy-dream-astronaut-night-1077863/

The Connection between the Unconscious Mind and the Conscious Mind

Sigmund Freud suggests that the unconscious mind is responsible for your dreams, as it represents your deepest thoughts, desires, and wishes. He stated that the thoughts and emotions you repress from the conscious mind show themselves in your dreams originating from your unconscious mind. According to a Harvard University experiment conducted by psychologist Daniel Wegner, repressing thoughts is futile because they will keep coming back in the form of dreams.

Your dreams aren't just based on your repressed thoughts but the thoughts you have in your waking life as well. The things you see, the emotions you feel, and anything your conscious mind experiences in your waking life are stored in your subconscious mind and will appear in your dreams.

Your subconscious drives the conscious mind's impulses and emotions. Interpreting your dreams gives you a better understanding of your subconscious mind, and, in turn, you'll learn who you are in your waking life. It is necessary to cultivate a relationship with it because it impacts every area of your life. Renowned psychiatrist Dr. Carl Jung believed that the subconscious mind could act as a teacher. You don't have to look outside yourself for guidance; just look within and pay attention to your dreams, and you'll discover answers and possibilities that are unclear to your conscious mind.

Now that you understand symbolism, metaphors, and the connection between the conscious and the subconscious mind, you'll learn about common symbols in dreams.

Archetypes – Ancient Primal Symbols

Carl Jung came up with the concept of archetypes. He defined them as primitive symbols passed down from generation to generation. He suggested that these patterns are universal and are stored in the unconscious. Archetypes can appear across cultures and mainly have shared meanings, unlike other symbols that depend on personal interpretations.

The Persona

The persona is the image you reflect to the world. It's who you are in your waking life. In your dreams, it often appears as the self, which can either look and act like you or be completely different. Even if it appears as another person, you'll be able to recognize that it's you. The persona is either who you wish you could be, or it could be a false image you use to trick or manipulate the people in your life.

When you see the persona in your dream, pay attention to what it says or does, as it can have a significant message for you.

The Self

The Self is your true potential and who you could become when you reach a higher consciousness. There are many symbols in your dreams that represent the self, such as a beautiful house, a warm summer day, a majestic lion, the sun, pearls, gold, gems, or art. The self is the part where all the inside conflict and juxtapositions inside of you take place.

The Shadow

The shadow represents the dark inside that you often dismiss and hide from the world. There is a part inside each person that they aren't proud of, so they repress it in their unconscious. It can be your anger, fears, or weaknesses. It usually appears in your dream as a dark creature like a murderer, bully, pervert, or stalker of the same gender as you. This dream will leave you feeling stressed or scared.

Your shadow is a part of you that you should embrace. It wants to heal you, awaken your deepest truth, and motivate you to change for the better. It often comes to you in a dream to confront you with a truth that you aren't ready to accept. So, pay attention to the messages it's trying to convey.

The Anima/Animus

The anima is the feminine side of every male, which is nurturing, creative, and intuitive. The animus represents the masculine attributes of every female, which are intellect, assertiveness, and strength. Females can see themselves growing beards in dreams, while males can see themselves wearing dresses. This dream urges you to accept the feminine or masculine side of your personality and express its different characteristics. The animus can also appear to you as a spear, tower, mountain, snake, lion, bull, or eagle. While the anima can be a ship, cave, water, ship, tiger, cat, cow, bear, or the earth.

The Divine Child

The divine child is the purest part of your personality that represents your child-like innocence. It is also a metaphor for your true potential and who you could become. It will appear to you as a child, baby, kitten, puppy, or any other baby animal.

The Old Wise Woman/Man

It is a teacher or guide who comes to you in a dream to encourage you to reach the highest level of awareness and put you on the right path. It also represents unconditional love. The old wise woman or man can appear to you as an authority figure, guru, doctor, magician, wizard, prophet, goddess, teacher, parent, grandparent, queen, or king. You can also see popular movie figures like Professor Dumbledore from Harry Potter, Merlin from the King Arthur story, Obi-Wan Kenobi from Star Wars, Gandalf in the Lord of the Rings, or the Fairy Godmother.

The Great Mother

The great mother is a nurturing figure like your mother or grandmother. She will appear to you in a dream to give you protection and love. However, she can sometimes have a negative meaning. For instance, she can be jealous and angry that you are growing and becoming an independent individual. This can represent your relationship with your mother, who is unhappy that you are growing up and leaving her. She can also appear as an evil witch or an ugly old woman, symbolizing dominance and seduction.

The Trickster

The trickster represents the immature part of your personality that refuses to grow. He symbolizes rebellion, but its purpose is to transform you and help you grow. It is the fun side that prevents you from taking life seriously. The trickster will appear to you in a dream whenever you face indecision or struggle with finding the right path in life. He can reveal your vulnerabilities, mock you, and make you uncomfortable enough to push you to change your way of thinking or ask questions rather than blindly following the rules. The trickster can appear in any shape or form, like a villain, jester, clown, magician, destroyer, fox, or fool.

Numbers

Numbers can have different meanings in your dream depending on the context and the number itself.

Numbers in the Skies

This dream indicates that you need to take a break and have some fun. You are neglecting your needs either for the sake of others or your career, and it's time to practice self-care.

Lottery Numbers

Dreaming of lottery numbers is a pleasant dream that symbolizes joy, freedom, success, and financial gain in your future.

Dates

Dates can be a reminder of a significant event, anniversary, or the birthday of a loved one. Dreaming of your birthdate symbolizes good fortune and success.

Phone Numbers

This dream could have a positive meaning, like success and growth, or a negative one, revealing unfinished business you need to complete.

Repeated Numbers

Repeated numbers like 555 can be messages from the universe to bring your attention to something from your past.

Meaning of Common Numbers

- **One:** New beginnings, growth, change, and manifestation. It invites you to look within for answers. The number eleven is a message from your guardian angel that they are by your side.

- **Two:** It is a sign that you have to make a decision that could affect your relationship or career significantly. It also symbolizes success and an exciting chapter in your life. The number twenty-two is a message from your guardian angel that they will provide guidance, so have faith.

- **Three:** It invites you to listen to your spirit guide and follow your intuition. It also signifies that you have always had spiritual guidance. Thirty-three symbolizes strength, positivity, optimism, and abundance.

- **Four:** It means your life is cluttered and in need of organization.

- **Five:** This number symbolizes achieving goals, work-life balance, satisfaction, and good health

- **Six:** It is an invitation to ignore the noise outside of you and look within.

- **Seven:** This is a message from the universe to say you'll overcome any obstacles because you are on the right path. It can also be a supportive sign from your guardian angel that you are making the right decisions.

- **Eight:** It is a sign that you are about to experience abundance, peace, and happiness.

- **Nine:** Nine symbolizes that you are about to discover your purpose in life.

Colors

Each color has a different meaning. However, they are open to personal interpretation. For instance, if you dream of a color you don't like, you should consider its negative meaning, but if you dream of one of your favorite colors, focus on its positive meaning.

Colors have different meanings in dreams.
https://unsplash.com/photos/jbtfM0XBeRc?utm_source=unsplash&utm_medium=referral&utm_content=creditShareLink

White
- Perfection
- Confidence
- Purity
- Faith
- Hope
- Enlightenment

Black
- Lack of faith
- Hopelessness
- Depression
- Guilt
- Anxiety
- Hate
- Fear
- Darkness

Red
- Luck
- Passion
- Sex
- Warning
- Anger

Blue
- Honesty
- Creativity
- Peacefulness
- Unhappiness
- Sadness
- Depression
- Wisdom
- Emotion

Green
- Inner healing
- Disconnection from nature
- Success
- Wealth
- Money
- Dissatisfaction
- Jealousy

Yellow
- Optimism
- Positivity
- Light
- Warmth

Orange
- Chasing your goals
- Abundance
- Ambition
- Energy

Purple
- Spiritual warning
- Psychic abilities
- Power
- Wealth
- A warning of a storm

Pink
- Desire
- Unconditional love
- Empathy
- Generosity
- Flirtation

Brown
- Materialism
- Comfort
- Domestic bliss
- Practicality

Feelings

Pay attention to how you feel in your dreams because each emotion is trying to tell you something.

Happiness

Happiness in dreams can reflect how you feel in your waking life. It can also compensate for negative feelings you experience in real life, like sadness, frustration, or stress.

Sadness

If you are sad or crying in your dream, you are overwhelmed by powerful emotions that manifest in your dreams. Seeing another sad person crying symbolizes a part of yourself that is grieving or feeling emotional.

Anger

Anger symbolizes your awareness of your suppressed emotions. It can also mean that you dislike a part of your personality. Anger can indicate that you are taking action and making serious changes in your life.

Fear and Anxiety

These are usually unpleasant dreams that indicate you are stressed, worried, and anxious in your real life. Anxiety in your dream is a message from your subconscious to look within because you are going through troubling emotions.

Disgust

Disgust symbolizes the change or transformation that is going on in your waking life. To interpret this dream better, focus on what's making you disgusted. Throwing up out of disgust indicates that you are struggling with quitting bad habits and letting go of negative thoughts. It can also mean cleansing your spirit and walking away from what doesn't serve you anymore.

Shame

You may be experiencing embarrassment in your waking life, and your subconscious is showing you how to handle the situation. This dream may also protect you from emotional stress or can be a warning that your environment is unsafe.

Objects

Sharp Objects

Dreaming of sharp objects means you need to look within to better understand who you are and make the necessary changes to be the best version of yourself. They also symbolize success, fame, achieving your goals, and making a real impact in the world.

Cursed Objects

This dream is a warning that you are in a dangerous situation and need to protect yourself. You may also have someone in your life who is manipulating you or forcing you to be someone you are not. It can also mean you are resilient and easily adapt to any situation.

Floating Objects

This dream indicates novelty in your life or that something amazing is about to happen. You are about to experience change, like adopting a pet or starting a family.

Objects Falling from the Sky

This is a sign that you need to rest and re-energize. You feel stagnant living in a boring routine, and your unconscious mind is telling you to do something different. It shows you are in need of a break or escape because you feel uncomfortable in your current situation. It can also be a symbol of your repressed emotions.

Inanimate Objects Coming to Life

This dream is trying to bring your attention to something you're neglecting in your waking life – like your relationship falling apart. If the object starts moving, this is a warning that someone or something is threatening you.

Moving Objects with Your Mind

If you are moving an object with your mind while feeling calm, you are proud of yourself and your accomplishments. Throwing objects at others while feeling hostile symbolizes self-defense.

Animals

Each animal represents a side of your personality, primitive desire, physical attributes, or sexual nature. Similar to colors, consider your personal feelings about the animal before interpreting your dream.

Apes

- Sexual nature
- Going crazy
- Falsehood
- Mischievousness
- Deception

Bats

- Demons
- Dirty environment

- Rebirth
- Unrealized potential
- Quitting old habits
- A vampire bat indicates someone in your life is sucking your self-confidence out of you.
- In China, dreaming of five bats is a symbol of joy, abundance, and good health.

Bear
- Resurrection
- Rebirth
- Death
- Strength
- Independence
- Introspection

Bull
- Power
- Strength
- Strong will
- Stubbornness
- Virility
- Sexual energy

Cat

Cats represent power and feminine energy.
https://unsplash.com/photos/mBRfYA0dYYE?utm_source=unsplash&utm_medium=referral&utm_content=creditShareLink

- Power
- Creativity
- Feminine energy
- Independence
- Bad luck
- Betrayal
- A black cat symbolizes fear or trusting your gut

Cow
- Blind obedience
- Maternal nature
- Motherhood
- Fertility

Dog
- Fidelity
- Protection
- Generosity
- Loyalty
- Feeling accepted

Symbols from Your Waking Life

Symbols that you see in your daily life can creep into your subconscious and appear in your dreams.

Clothes
- Concern about your image
- Feeling unattractive
- Low self-esteem

Cross
- A representation of your cultural and religious beliefs
- Sacrifice
- Redemption
- Hope

- Confusion
- Guidance
- Protection

Food
- Excess
- Guilt
- Indulgence
- Pleasure
- Symbolize your relationship with your body
- Metaphor for knowledge

Hair
- Social status
- Self-image
- Feeling creative
- Rebellious
- Vulnerable
- Powerful
- Confident
- Attractive

Time, Seasons, and Weather

Time
- If it's daytime in your dream, it represents a new path and rebirth.
- Noon represents midlife.
- Evening represents overcoming difficulty and moving on to the next stage of your life.
- If your dream takes place at night, it signifies revealing things that are hidden.

Seasons
- Winter represents introspection, endings, sorting, and preparing for what's to come.
- Spring is an invitation to assess your relationships with others and yourself. It is also a symbol of new beginnings, youth, and childhood.
- Fall represents transformation and wisdom. It is also a reminder to acknowledge your success. This dream can be a warning to prepare for hardships.
- Summer signifies learning, energy, development, growth, relaxation, success, and taking a step back to see the big picture.

Weather
- Rain symbolizes complicated situations, loss, peace, obstacles, harmony, or prosperity. If the rain floods your house, you'll experience harsh times for which you are unprepared.
- A rainbow is a sign of happiness, joy, success, hope, and new beginnings.
- Wind symbolizes intellect, knowledge, and a promise of better days. While a hurricane means there are difficult days on the horizon.
- Heat warns you against making hasty decisions and is a sign that you are going to fight your boss or partner.
- Lightning symbolizes the joy you'll share with someone special.
- Thunder signifies spending time with family or changing jobs.
- Breeze means you'll experience betrayal from someone close to you.

Each dream symbol has a different meaning behind it. Before interpreting, consider your cultural and religious background, feelings toward the symbol, and context. The next chapters will discuss dream locations, themes, and patterns so you can understand and analyze dream symbols better.

Chapter 4: Decoding Common Dreamscapes

Exploring dreamscapes is like entering into a new reality. The subconscious mind crafts complex, intricate environments that stimulate wonder, awe, and sometimes excruciating fear. Different cultures and philosophies understand these environments in varying ways. Ancient animist traditions say that dreamscapes are otherworldly realms, so when you sleep, it is like interdimensional traveling. The Jungian view of dreamscapes is that the collective unconscious of human beings, past and present, is expressed through common themes and motifs. Common dream environments are an ancestral inheritance that can reveal deep insights into your psychology.

    Whether you look at it through the lens of interdimensional travel or as an expression of the subconscious, the entire universe of a dream is constructed mentally. There are no elements that are irrelevant. Every meticulous detail of your experience is communicated through symbols and iconography. Furthermore, your ancestral memory coded in your genetics is unveiled in these dream realms. Therefore, popular archetypes of dream environments are shared across cultures that have little to no influence on one another. By analyzing the environmental context of a dream, you get a more comprehensive picture of your subconscious.

    A dreamscape is the entire environment or world in which your dream is taking place. Dreamscapes can be composed of unique color palettes and laws of physics that widely contrast with waking reality. The mind-bending paintings of Salvador Dali are an incredible visual representation of how dreamscapes deviate from the norm. Furthermore, the meaning of dreamscapes can be interpreted according to how you feel. For example, you may dream of being in a vast, dark void. However, whether you feel fear or discomfort frames how the dreamscape is received. Dreamscapes often reflect the waking world. However, there are subtle changes that make them impactful.

The subconscious sends you important messages by breaking down the limitations of what the rational mind can perceive and explain. It's as if your subconscious is telling you secrets that you cannot access through ordinary experiences. The subconscious becomes the storyteller. As much as the characters and plot of the story communicate, the set and setting are equally significant. Scriptwriters and authors spend countless hours on world-building because the setting determines the surrounding context of any story that is being told. In films and fictional books, certain genre conventions exist that show early on in the story what type of events may occur. A dreamscape is like a genre convention for a dream. Different stories may be told according to your personal experiences. However, commonalities emerge through the environment.

Dreams can help you decipher various aspects of decisions or paths you are walking while you are awake. A dreamscape will help point you to the area of your life that needs attention. Therefore, dreamscapes act as a lens through which you interpret objects or events taking place in a dream. Paying attention to your surroundings in a dream provides an overview into the broader context of a current situation, problem, or position you are in related to a part of your life. Understanding dreamscapes lets you uncover that extra layer of interpretation that can give you some crucial pieces to the puzzle that the subconscious puts together.

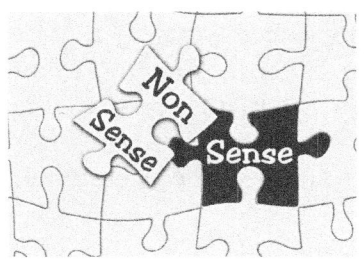

To interpret a dream, you need to understand the dreamscape, even if it feels like nonsense.
https://pixabay.com/illustrations/puzzle-sense-nonsense-sensible-432569/

Landscapes

Landscapes are meant to show you a wider panorama of what you are going through. It's like your mind is telling you to zoom out and look at the bigger picture. A landscape can only be seen from a distance, so taking a step back for the analysis of dreams containing landscapes reveals a far wider perspective. It can highlight where there is a need to address bigger issues in your life, like your career, family, or even deeply held belief systems. Paying attention to the types of landscapes in the dream will show you your perception of the broad sphere the dream is covering.

A desert landscape may be an indication that baroness is a certain part of your life. Let's say you dream about your office being in the middle of the desert. This may show you that your current employment is not fulfilling. Another way to look at the same situation is the need to put more energy into your work. Dryness implies that there is a need to be nourished. When a desert landscape appears, know that something is missing. The details of what you are doing in the desert or what is happening will show you where the lack is. For example, if you dream about family members in the desert, this means that there is a lack in your relationship or your family life.

The opposite of the desert landscape is the wetland or forest landscape. This is an indication of abundance. When you see a wetland landscape, your subconscious mind is telling you that the path you have chosen to take will yield fruit. If the backdrop to your dream is a wetland environment, you can infer that success is on the way. The abundance can be woven into many parts of your life and is not necessarily monetary. It could be an abundance of love from a partner or friend or even an abundance of time if you are working a demanding job.

Another landscape that often appears in the dream world is a mountainous region. Mountains represent obstacles. If you are at the top of the mountain, it shows that you have overcome a hurdle in your life, whereas if you are in the valley, it shows that you still have obstacles to face. The number of mountains and the weather are further symbols of the kinds of obstacles you are facing. Moreover, the size of the mountains is also relevant. A huge mountain may show that you need to ask for help because the obstacle is overwhelming, while many smaller mountains show a long, bumpy road ahead. Cold weather indicates that you may have to face obstacles in isolation, and pleasant weather or rain shows that you have the help you can rely on. Mountains can also represent revelation or new insight. In the biblical tradition, Moses received the Israelite law on a mountain. Mountains are land that is close to the sky, so mountain peaks can represent the acquisition of higher information.

A coastline is an interesting landscape to encounter in a dream because it represents balance, duality, or the clashing of opposing forces. On the coastline, the land meets the water. The land represents your physical or material existence, such as your finances and resources, while the water represents your spiritual or emotional life. If the water is destroying the land, it shows that you need to put more focus on your material reality, but if the shore is large and the water is far in the distance, it shows that you are neglecting your emotional or spiritual needs.

Houses, Buildings, and Construction Sites

Cityscapes, buildings, houses, and construction sites are related to the material world. Man-made buildings are symbolic of wealth, status, and ambition. Any construction needs to be built, so the dream shows effort on your part. This may be a calling to put in more effort, or it may show that you are already working hard. Like the other dreamscapes discussed before, the condition of the house, building, or construction reveals the state of your existing material reality. Furthermore, the type of construction shows which area of life your dream is unpacking.

Construction sites still in progress - this refers to a new material venture you are working on. This new venture could be a new job you've started or even a business you are planning to begin. A construction site can also refer to an investment that you've made. A broken construction site may show that you are close to giving up on a particular mission, or it may tell you to get out while you can because it won't succeed. A chaotic construction site shows that your new venture is uncertain or unstable and that you need to put measures in place to bring in more order. A neat, clean, and efficient construction site shows that things are running smoothly, and it would be best to stick to your current path.

A house deals with realities closer to home. Since you live in your house and the structure is man-made, dreams about houses reveal material concerns close to you. If you see a neighborhood with many houses, the dream refers to your community concerns. This community does not have to be where you live, just a community that you are a part of. For example, you may have a passion for clothes, so you would be a part of the fashion community. If there is one house, or you are inside of a house, this is a more closely held link like family or even your own life as an individual. Broken or dirty houses show a need for change or correction, while pristine homes show that you are doing well. Unfinished homes or empty homes indicate that you still have some work to do.

A full cityscape deals with your ambition. This is aligned with your goals and dreams in a broader sense. Cities are where money is made and are economic hubs. Therefore, the ambition that cityscapes symbolize is directly tied to your career path. A dark city shows that you have some uncertainty concerning your career, while a brightly lit city shows that you hold a more positive view of your current career trajectory. Dilapidated cities show that you have no career motivation at the moment. A city under construction shows that you are growing and building your career vision. A busy city shows that your vision is in full swing. However, if the city is chaotic, it may be an indication that some adjustments need to be made because your vision is under threat.

Cityscapes are related to ambition.
https://unsplash.com/photos/wpU4veNGnHg?utm_source=unsplash&utm_medium=referral&utm_content=creditShareLink

Water

In the Shamanic traditions of South Africa, healers, or "Sangomas," interpret the prevalence of water in a dream as a sign that one has a spiritual calling, as well as indicating a need for cleansing. Being submerged in an underwater world may show that you need to detox your life or have a complete overhaul. The main motifs that are attached to water are emotion, spirit, life, and cleansing. Amongst Native American groups, there is a view that water is the giver of life. This commonly occurs in many cultures because people can live weeks without food but only a few days without water. Furthermore, scientifically, the origin of life began in water.

The emotional world is central to the symbolism of water in dreams. The way the water behaves reflects your emotional state at the time. For example, rough seas or violent storms may indicate a period of turmoil, while calm, serene environments reflect a peaceful emotional state. Since water is closely tied to your emotional state, the hygiene of the water also has an impact. Clean water sends a different message. Clean water shows that there is clarity or cleansing taking place, while dirty water shows a feeling of guilt or a general heaviness.

The archetype of life is also closely related to water. The creator goddess Nun in ancient Egyptian mythology is the chaotic primordial waters from which all life emerges. Therefore, water in a dream can also indicate an upcoming life shift. This may be a change in your partner, career, or belief system. Water that represents a new birth tends to be vast and dark. The darkness represents the unknown, as well as potential. A newborn baby is filled with potential because nobody knows what the baby is going to grow up to be. Similarly, diverting to a new path is also filled with potential because it strays from the predictable outcomes you are accustomed to.

Water in a dreamscape can take multiple forms. The shapable and moldable properties of water allow it to exist in the abstract. This abstract nature of water is why it is often related to emotion and spirituality. Water comes in the form of rivers, lakes, and ponds. The ocean is the deep unknown. Whenever you dream about the ocean, you can see it as a sign to do some soul-searching and introspection. If the ocean waters are rough, it shows that the journey is going to bring negative emotions to the surface. Rough seas indicate that you should address your trauma so that you can heal. The ocean is a combination of water and salt. Salt is often used to disinfect, and water is used to clean. When salt is used to disinfect a wound, it burns and causes pain. Therefore, dreaming about the sea directs you to a painful yet necessary healing journey.

Nature, Plants, and Animals

Nature is a difficult construction to comprehend because so much falls under this category. Moreover, nature is what keeps all the organisms on earth alive. Interacting with nature, like plants and animals in dreamscapes, could mean several different things. Since dreamscapes are the setting of a broader vision, the types of plants and animals in a dreamscape will be more a part of the world than one-on-one interactions. In a dreamscape, how the plants and animals receive you is the key to interpretation.

Plants are related to growth. A single plant may be very specific to a particular relationship or event in your life, but plants in a dreamscape are more aligned with a wider aspect of your reality. If the environment you are in is filled with invasive weeds, it shows that there are things (or even people) you need to remove from your life. Smaller plants, like seedlings, show that you are at the beginning of a growth period. Larger trees symbolize great growth in a sector of your life. The condition of the plants is significant as well. Dead trees or plants show that you are on the wrong path or you are stuck in a rut – which means you must make drastic changes. Dead plants may also represent the end of a season, meaning that it may be time to let go of a part of your life you once held dear. Pay attention to your emotions in the dream because this could help with interpretation. If you are comfortable in a dead forest, you need to let go. If you are uncomfortable in a dead forest, it is a sign that you may be completely off track.

Wild animals in dreams deal with your primal self, while domesticated animals are more related to your cultivated or engineered identity. Your primal self refers to basic needs like food, shelter, clothing, and interpersonal relationships. Your created identity comprises the secondary labels you embody, like culture or titles. How the animals behave will show you more about your primal or engineered self. For example, if the animals look malnourished, it's an indication you need to put work into developing that part of your character. If the animals are aggressive, it indicates that conflict is plaguing you. If these animals appear deformed or extremely otherworldly, it may indicate that you are pretending to be something that you are not.

Social Interactions, Parties, Meetings, and Gatherings

Crowds in dreams deal with the social contracts that humanity lives under. This includes culture, religion, race, nationality, and the multitude of other groups we belong to. Different kinds of social interactions will indicate which societal contracts are being highlighted by your subconscious. Parties symbolize friendship, and formal meetings symbolize your career partnerships. When it comes to dreamscapes with crowds in them, the direction the crowd is moving is a key focus aspect. Is the crowd coming towards you or walking away from you? How fast is the crowd moving? Are you trying to get closer to the crowd, or are you running away?

Crowds deal with the social contracts humanity lives under.
https://unsplash.com/photos/sUXXO3xPBYo?utm_source=unsplash&utm_medium=referral&utm_content=creditShareLink

One of the basic human needs is connection. Humans are social, so everybody cares what groups think about them to varying degrees. Although you may be consciously trying to dissociate from your group identity, your subconscious mind, where your purest desires dwell, will show you how you exist within a group. When you are chasing a crowd, it means you are seeking a group identity. This may be a propeller to join a social group or to reconnect with existing groups.

When a group in your dream seems hostile or violent, this may be an indication that you are feeling alienated. Maybe your values have shifted, and you no longer see this group as beneficial for you. So, if you combine the context of the group and their behavior, the interpretation of the dream becomes clearer. Let's say you are dreaming that you are at a party. This shows the recreational or friendship side of your social life. The crowd at the party may be hostile to you, and decorations may seem out of place. This shows that you no longer align with your current friend group. You still have strong positive feelings for them, and that's why you are at a party, but you may have outgrown them, or you are just at a different stage in life. Your friends may still be going out and partying while you are raising a family.

This same kind of interpretation could work across multiple different groups. Maybe you are running after a group of people in business suits. This shows that you are looking to get into a certain financial group. Maybe you want to be upwardly mobile and enter a new financial class. The key to interpreting what a group symbolizes is the analysis of what kind of group it is and how it reacts to your presence.

Chapter 5: Dream Themes and Their Symbolism

Dreams often have common themes experienced by many people. When discussing dreams, you'll often bring up a dream scenario and hear people comment about how they, too, have had similar dreams. For example, many people have had a dream where they are falling, and they wake up just before they hit the ground. Shared cultural experiences, as well as shared human evolution encoding in your cultural psyche, means you often have similar dreams to your peers. Humans have mutual fears, desires, and experiences that influence the contexts of dream themes and their symbolism. Therefore, you can draw from psychological data and intuitive emotions how these themes can be interpreted. With an understanding of cultural development and the commonalities among humans, you can accurately gauge the significance of thematic occurrences in dreams.

Arguments

Dreams about arguments can be a sign that emotions of anger or resentment are suppressed.
https://www.pexels.com/photo/man-and-woman-wearing-brown-leather-jackets-984950/

Dreams about arguments can be a sign of suppressed emotions like anger or resentment. Since these emotions are not being expressed in your daily life, your mind finds a way to bring them to your attention. Arguments represent an internal conflict that stems from invalidating your own feelings. Holding in your anger is like creating a highly pressurized, sealed container being pumped full of water. Eventually, the container will explode. If this explosion does not occur while you are awake, your mind finds ways to release the pressure while you sleep. Pay attention to whom you are arguing with in the dream and what the argument is about. These will point you in the direction of your unresolved emotional issues. When you dream about arguments, it is indicative that you need to express your emotions and communicate your thoughts because you feel as if you are not being heard.

Being Chased

Few things are as terrifying as being chased. The discomfort this dream creates is already an indication that there is negativity attached to being chased. Dreaming of it means that you are either feeling overwhelmed with your responsibilities or that you are stressed. Moreover, this dream could also mean that you are anxious about an upcoming event or that there is something you are avoiding in your life. Being chased is a primal experience that relates to the predator and prey dynamic. If you are being chased, it puts you in the position of prey that will do anything to escape. So, dreaming about being chased is closely related to avoidance. This may be a responsibility you are trying to avoid or even a conversation you are evading. This avoidance could even be related to a person, place, or behavior that you are trying to distance yourself from.

Falling

This is one of the more common dreams that many people report having. The fear of falling is incredibly human. The primate past of humans before descending from the treetops to the open plains means that falling puts our evolutionary ancestors in extreme danger. This fear of falling is so ingrained into the human genetic code that one of the first fears that infants develop is a fear of falling. Dreaming about falling highlights a feeling of anxiety created by a lack of control. Another common interpretation of falling in a dream is taking a risk or feeling like you have no support. This feeling of being unsupported related to falling can be traced back to infancy when a baby relies on their mother to hold onto them to make sure they do not fall. Therefore, if you constantly dream of falling, it is necessary to look into the risks you are taking and the support system you rely on.

Teeth Falling Out

Losing teeth is related to two key aspects in the human life cycle, namely, a toddler losing baby teeth to make way for their adult teeth or when someone is getting old. Any other time that any individual loses teeth, it is either related to injury or illness. Teeth falling out is also one of the more common dream themes, with about 39% of the population having had this dream (Summer and Singh, 2023). Since teeth loss is related to aging and decreased health in the waking world, dreaming about tooth loss either indicates a fear of losing someone or something, as well as anxiety attached to your personal health condition. The loss of teeth is linked to feelings of distress, so dreaming about tooth loss is seldom a good sign for your mental health and emotional well-being.

Hair Loss

Dreams of losing your hair come in two forms, namely shaving all your hair off and, secondly, experiencing your hair falling out. The more simplistic interpretation of this dream, which is often accurate, is the fear of losing your hair. Hair loss in a dream could have several different meanings. It could mean that you are going through a transition in your life. Hair loss is also related to aging, so losing hair in a dream could indicate a fear of getting old, as well as a fear of death. Hair is closely tied to beauty, so dreaming of losing your hair could indicate that you feel like you are losing your attractiveness. It can also be related to stress; as the saying goes, "I'm so stressed, I'm pulling my hair out."

Visits from Deceased Loved Ones

Many cultures attach a spiritual significance to being visited by deceased loved ones. In some traditional African belief systems, as well as philosophies that stem from the Americas, there is a belief that the ancestral realm is alive, so dreaming of deceased loved ones could mean that your ancestors are trying to open a line of communication to contact you. From a more psychological perspective, dreaming about deceased people shows that you are processing grief. A lot of people suppress their emotions in waking life, but the subconscious mind will facilitate the grieving process while you sleep. Dreaming about a lost loved one shows the high level of attachment you have to the individual and the central role they played in your life. Therefore, dreaming of the deceased is the mind's way of processing the death and the reality that the individual is no longer available to connect with physically.

Flying

Flying is a symbol of independence and freedom. The United States is a country that glorifies freedom. Therefore, much of the country's symbolism uses the iconography of the eagle, which is a bird that flies higher than many other birds. Flying could either show that you desire freedom and independence or that you already feel free and independent. Thus, a flying dream must be interpreted in the context of your life and your experiences. Flying is a pleasant dream to have and is not often coupled with feelings of distress. Flying in a dream can also be interpreted as a representation of joy, increased confidence, and success.

When you fly, you are at a higher level, meaning that you perceive yourself as someone who is excelling. If you perceive yourself as someone free and successful, this will inevitably be coupled with increased confidence.

Car Crashes

A car crash is a traumatic experience. What makes car crashes unique in terms of dream symbolism is how dramatically and suddenly they can occur. At one moment, you are feeling safe and calm, then in a split second, you are in this loud, chaotic crash. Therefore, car crashes symbolize abrupt and messy endings. A car moves fast, but when it crashes, it comes to a quick stop. The results of the crash can be violent and gruesome. Therefore, the end that you are anticipating or that you have experienced was not a clean break. The dream of a car crash means that there will be conflict in whatever is coming to an end. This may be a messy break-up or a split from a job that does not end amicably. It can also mean that a friendship is coming to an end, and there will be a fight attached to that ending. A crash is a sudden end instead of a smooth transition.

Warfare

When you dream of warfare, it can either represent confusion or it can also represent a big conflict in your life. When nation-states or different groups go to war, it is usually because a conflict couldn't be resolved through diplomacy or conversation. Both sides were unable to compromise or acquiesce to the demands of their opposition. This inability to reach an agreement manifests itself in chaos. The chaos of war is what is symbolized when you dream of warfare. Furthermore, the confusion and chaos that is caused stem from your inability to compromise, or maybe the opposite is true, and you are being too agreeable. Therefore, dreaming of war is a reflection of conflict and chaos caused by weak boundaries or perceptions that are too rigid. If you are dreaming about warfare, examine the conflicts in your life or the positions you hold through the lens of the consequences that these positions cause for your well-being.

Apocalyptic Dreams

During the Covid-19 pandemic, many people reported having apocalyptic dreams. Apocalyptic dreams are related to the end of the world. This can include dreams about natural disasters like earthquakes, an asteroid hitting Earth, or even man-made events like nuclear destruction. Apocalyptic dreams indicate a great unease in your life that feels like you can't overcome it. These dreams can also symbolize a feeling of helplessness. The reason many people experience these kinds of dreams during pandemics is the combination of feeling like the world is going to end, as well as the feeling that they are unable to control their destiny. Thus, apocalyptic dreams deal with loss of control in a way that largely impacts your life. If you are experiencing apocalyptic dreams, you must begin re-evaluating different aspects of your existence.

Being Naked in Public

Dreams about nakedness indicate that you have a fear of being exposed. People usually cover themselves with clothing. For most individuals, when someone sees them naked, especially someone they are not close to or intimate with, it will cause some embarrassment. Therefore, clothes are covers that hide your shame. When people dream of being naked in public, it means that they are hiding something in their waking life. People keep secrets for many reasons, including for their benefit and to protect others. The fear of getting exposed gets revealed in a dream by public nudity. Everyone in the dream is seeing what is hidden. You may be keeping secrets from a friend or your family for whatever reason. This dream is an indication of the guilt that one feels by hiding certain aspects of one's life.

Snakes

Snakes can symbolize wisdom or slyness.
https://www.pexels.com/photo/brown-snake-106690/

One of the most common animals that people encounter in dreams is snakes. The symbolism of snakes has taken various forms throughout the millennia. Snakes often are used to symbolize wisdom or slyness. Another symbol that snakes are used for is transformation. Therefore, when you encounter snakes in dreams, it means that you are gaining new insight that is facilitating profound transformation. In some African traditions, dreaming about snakes is a sign that you have to begin the initiation process to become a traditional healer. In these cultures, traditional healers are seen as the custodians of hidden or higher information. Therefore, the motif of a snake representing transformational knowledge re-emerges through the process of initiation that will be life-changing for the initiate. As counterintuitive as it seems, dreaming about snakes is often a good sign that new beginnings are approaching.

Spiders

Next to snakes, spiders are another one of the most commonly encountered creatures in dreams. Spiders spin webs to catch their prey. Therefore, spiders are related to the feeling of being trapped, as well as deceit. A saying that you may have heard before is, "She spun a web of lies." When people tell lies, especially impactful lies that have big consequences, they need to keep telling further lies to cover up or create an elaborate story. This results in the need to detangle the lies, like when prey gets caught in a web and needs to detangle itself. Dreaming of spiders means that you are suspicious that someone is deceiving you or can indicate that you have been deceitful. The West African deity Anansi appears as a spider, and he is a trickster god. The symbol of a spider in dreams represents deceitful behavior to manipulate people.

Using the Toilet or Being Unable to Find a Bathroom

The imagery of a toilet in dreams can be analyzed in multiple ways. If you are using the toilet in a dream, it is an indication that you are experiencing some form of release in your waking life. If you are unable to find a toilet, it means that you are holding on to unprocessed emotions; however, you are seeking a way to delve into these misunderstood feelings. Toilets work with water, so seeking a toilet could also show that you have a desire to cleanse. This cleansing could be a reform of your behavior or letting go of what does not serve you. Toilets are also used in private most of the time. This shows that the processing of the emotions that you are going through is an individual or very personal issue. Furthermore, because toilets are private, seeking a toilet in a dream could also communicate the desire for isolation.

Giving Birth

Giving birth ushers new life onto the planet. In a symbolic sense, giving birth in dreams means that a creative opportunity is coming to fruition. Artists often call their work their "babies." Much like giving birth, a creative project takes a lot of effort. The project does not only need to be artistic; it could be the beginning of a new relationship or the start of a new business. Giving birth in a dream means new opportunities or transformations are on the horizon. If you are giving birth in a dream, it is a sign to take the risk on the project you are about to begin or make that new life change you have been putting off. Giving birth in a dream highlights that the process of starting this new journey could be painful, but there is a payoff in the end.

Being in School

Dreaming of school represents an opportunity to learn. This could mean that you are in the process of learning a new language or skill, starting a new job, or learning a new life lesson. The school environment and your relationship with education are also important to the interpretation. If the school is in a broken state, it could mean you are learning lessons that will not benefit you. A larger school indicates that you are learning a big lesson that will impact your life. A dirty school may mean that the lessons you are learning could hurt yourself and others. The central symbol of the school in dreams has to do with education. How this education shows up is how different variables for interpretation are considered.

Running Late

The dream of running late presents itself in various forms. You could be late for your transport, late for school, late to a function, or late for work. When you are late, there is stress and anxiety attached to it because you have to rush. Thus, dreaming about being late indicates that there is a lot of stress or pressing anxiety in your waking life. Furthermore, the anxiety and stress that you are experiencing is related to specific events or circumstance. What you are late for will point you in the direction of the circumstance from which the stress stems. If you are late for a party, your social life is giving you stress; if you are late for work, your career is causing anxiety.

Drowning

When you dream of drowning, it means that your commitments, obligations, and responsibilities are becoming overwhelming. These dreams often happen at stressful points in life where there is a lot of turmoil. For example, you may have this dream if you have just started a family and feel unstable in trying to maintain a work-life balance. A dream of drowning shows that you need help with your obligations because the only way a drowning victim is saved is when someone assists them.

Dreams about Someone Stalking or Watching You

Sometimes, people dream about being watched by shadowy figures. The figure may be standing in the corner of the room, or it may be following you around. When you dream that someone is watching you, it symbolizes that there is vulnerability and insecurity in your waking life. This is not the kind of vulnerability you share with a loved one and feel safe expressing. The vulnerability symbolized in this dream is a feeling that you are being taken advantage of or being manipulated. Furthermore, when you are being stalked by a figure you can't see, it highlights the uncertainty and fear you feel about being vulnerable.

Silent Screams

Many people report a feeling of fear of something happening, like a monster or some sort of adversary, and when they attempt to call out for help, no sound comes out. This silent scream shows you feel your voice is not being heard. Either you feel like you are being ignored, or you feel you have no control over various aspects of your life. The object, person, or thing that is causing you to scream is an indication of what or which aspect of your life you feel voiceless. These silent screams can be very traumatizing and scary when they occur, showing a deep desire to express yourself. Silent screams mean that you are either expressing yourself insufficiently or that someone is not taking your words seriously.

Chapter 6: Dream Interpretation Methods

It is widely known that dream interpretation has been used as a therapeutic tool for eons. With the right approach, dreams can serve as a self-awareness resource when digging deeper into one's subconscious and emotional state. By exploring diverse methods of dream analysis and interpretation, this chapter encourages you to develop your toolkit of interpretation techniques and gain insight into the rich and complex world of dream symbolism. It outlines different dream analysis methods, including Jungian dream analysis, Freud's psychoanalytic approach, cognitive dream interpretation, and intuitive reflection approaches like visualization, journaling, and more.

Dreams can help you become more self-aware.
https://unsplash.com/photos/D44kHt8Ex14?utm_source=unsplash&utm_medium=referral&utm_content=creditShareLink

Jungian Dream Analysis

Jungian dream analysis examines archetypal symbols, dream analysis techniques, and the exploration of personal and collective subconscious themes. It relies on the idea that dreams enable you to reach your subconscious through your conscious mind. This method introduces the concepts of anima/animus, shadow, and the process of individuation, the archetypes developed by Jung based on his research of symbolism in relation to the human psyche. As the father of psychoanalysis, Jung developed the concept of the Ego, the entity formed of awareness and conscious thoughts. However, these thoughts dwarf what's hidden in the subconscious, and this is where dream analysis comes in handy.

The shadow is the murkiest side of your personality. It's also the most accessible and easiest to experience in a dream. Your subconscious mind will usually readily reveal it in the form of dark/forbidden dream experiences or symbols, or you may encounter your shadow in your dreams as another person, usually of the same gender as you. The anima embodies feminine traits and tendencies found in the male subconscious. Likewise, the animus personifies male characteristics and tendencies, appearing in the female subconscious. These two are even more hidden than the shadow and are rarely realized in waking life, although they may appear in dreams. They take the form of a person who is a caring one in the case of the anima and a rational one in the case of the animus. Dream encounters with the shadow, anima, or animus inspire thoughts and emotions you would never believe you had in waking life. This culminates in a deep awareness of the self (the summation of your conscious and subconscious experiences), enabling you to use dreams to reveal your hidden personality traits and work toward self-realization.

Here is how to use Jungian dream analysis:

1. Find a quiet and comfortable place without distractions to recall your dreams.
2. Once you feel relaxed in your mind and body, recall your dreams and start analyzing them. Have an open mind as you interpret your dream experiences.
3. Because dream experiences aren't meant to be literally interpreted, you'll need to link them to what's happening to you internally (what your conscious mind is aware of). This could be

any sensation you feel or anything you perceive within your body with your senses.

4. Reflect on the different dream elements. You can write them down to analyze them faster. After noting them, consider what you think they mean. Consider what the dream images, experiences, or symbols may be trying to convey to you. Look at them from different perspectives to get a more profound insight into their meaning.

5. Make a note of any recurring symbols or patterns. To do this, you might need to analyze several subsequent dreams to see if they have anything in common. Some of the symbols or patterns might have personal significance. Make sure you examine them thoroughly so you don't miss anything.

6. After identifying frequently occurring symbols or patterns in your dreams, consider what they might mean, too. Is there anything specific they might be trying to tell you? Besides this, you can ask yourself some of the following questions when analyzing your dream:

    - How did you feel after waking up from a dream?
    - Besides the details that caught your attention, what else did you observe in your dream?
    - Did you hear a specific sound, music, or someone's voice in your dream?
    - Did any person or animal appear in your dream?
    - What happened during your dream experience?
    - How did you feel during your dream experience?

7. Take some time to reflect on what you learned after asking yourself these questions. It's a good idea to jot down any insights in your journal, including emotions and thoughts you might have about your dream experiences after answering the questions. You can even add little drawings to symbolize a particularly insightful part.

Some dream meanings will be surprising because the subconscious doesn't send messages the conscious mind is aware of. However, there are a few factors to consider when finalizing the dream interpretation. For example, insightful interpretation is not self-inflating or self-congratulatory because you'll rarely learn information that's all positive and without a hint of negativity. Likewise, if you reach the conclusion that your dream is about blaming others for your misfortune, your interpretation is probably faulty. Your dream experiences give insight into yourself and not anyone else. Any other person who appears in your dreams represents a part of yourself.

Alternatively, you can share the content of your dreams with others. Telling your friend, family member, or therapist about your dream experiences may enable you to gain even more powerful insights.

According to the Jungian dream interpretation method, another option to learn is to amplify the symbolism in your dreams. To do this, you'll need to research the significance of the image, experience, or symbol that stood out in your dream. When doing this, consider your personal link to the symbols, their cultural meanings, and archetypal significance separately.

Freud's Psychoanalytic Approach

Freud's psychoanalytic approach is geared toward uncovering the significance of dream symbols, latent content, and the interpretation of dreams as reflections of repressed desires, conflicts, and unresolved experiences. The method is based on Freud's concepts of dream work, censorship, and wish fulfillment.

The roots of Freud's dream analysis can be found in the belief that you must express your desires and fulfill your dreams and wishes. Dreams are the gateway to the subconscious, which often hides a set of surprising traits. These could be infantile and irrational behavior, primitive thoughts, or other instinctual expressions of one's personality. According to Freud, all these represent unwanted or repressed desires, which can come to fruition only in dreams. Others may find repressed aggressive tendencies or sexual desires revealed in their dreams. Dreams could also be how your subconscious wants to resolve repressed issues, whether related to unwanted experiences and feelings and aggressive impulses or not.

Initially, Freud believed dreams to be short, fleeting experiences, and this is a theory that has since been debunked. People experience dreams of different lengths, although longer ones are easier to interpret. This applies particularly to dreams you experience before waking. According to the Freudian approach, most of your dreams are about the events you experienced the day before. While you don't have to limit yourself to the exact day, this method is most valuable for interpreting dreams related to past events.

Dreams embody the fulfillment of your wishes. What you see yourself do or say in your dreams may be what you can't do or say in your waking life. Even when you act out of anxiety or feel punished in your dreams, it stems from wish fulfillment, according to this approach. Dreams provide significant psychological insight into your subconscious, even if the dreams seem random and more related to mythical or religious concepts than your everyday life.

Freud distinguished between the latent (the hidden psychological meaning) and the manifested content of one's dreams (what you remember after waking up). The manifested version is often a version that has been distorted by the conscious mind, representing a different format of the wish waiting to be fulfilled. By contrast, the latent content is the wish in its purest form.

Freud introduced the concept of dream work, which denotes the effort your subconscious makes to the true significance of your dreams by converting them into something more pleasing or acceptable and less disturbing. For example, it may combine several meanings into one, making you think your dreams represent one thing when, in fact, they mean something else, or your mind may shift emotional significance from one experience, symbol, object, or person to another. In the best case, it will only display thoughts, feelings, or actions through symbols, making you put in an effort to decipher them.

Sigmund Freud developed several methods to reveal the latent content of dreams. Below are the most popular ones.

Dream Analysis

Dream analysis refers to a detailed review of your dreams. It's often performed by therapists, where the professional and the patient work together to decipher the latter's dreams. This involves analyzing the manifest content (by reviewing the actual dream experience) and considering what the dreams or their parts could reveal about the latent content (the patient's unconscious desires or repressed emotions and conflicts). That said, you can analyze your own dreams following the same method by first examining what you saw, heard, or otherwise perceived in your dreams and then drawing conclusions about their meaning and relation to repressed content in your subconscious. For example, you may uncover that they relate to a hidden desire or unfulfilled wish you believed to be long forgotten because you thought it would never come true.

Interpreting Symbols

According to Freud, dream symbols have universal meanings. Exploring symbolism occurring in your dreams through this approach might provide sufficient knowledge to decipher the significance of your dream experiences. However, it's necessary to emphasize that the meaning of symbols can vary from one person to another, and individual associations can't be discarded either. Even Freud affirmed that general symbols are more personal to the dreamer rather than having an all-inclusive meaning. In other words, you can't interpret what your dream symbolizes without considering your circumstances.

The symbols in your dreams are related to your circumstances.
https://pixabay.com/illustrations/unordered-chaos-3192273/

Possible Repression

Because repressed desires and conflicts often emerge in dreams, understanding what you might be pushing to the back of your mind could help you to interpret the dream's latent content. To do this, reflect on the dream experience and think about whether it reminds you of something you're trying to hide. This takes practice and time, as the mind is really good at repressing unwanted thoughts and feelings.

Cognitive Dream Interpretation

This form of dream interpretation clarifies how dreams can reflect cognitive patterns, emotional states, and creative problem-solving strategies. Cognitive dream interpretation was first introduced by a behavioral psychologist called Calvin Hall in his book entitled Cognitive Theory of Dreaming. Hall researched the cognitive effects of dreaming and performed a quantitative analysis of dream experiences. Based on his insights, cognitive dream interpretation asserts that dream imagery embodies one's thoughts. Any thought lurking in your subconscious will be displayed as a visual concept in your dreams, allowing hidden thoughts, desires, and notions to become visible and known to your conscious. Dreams can reveal how you envision your life deep inside you, even if you weren't consciously aware of this concept. According to the cognitive approach, dreams represent random thoughts brought together, and it takes time to sort them out and decipher them.

Here is how to reveal the way you see your world through cognitive dream interpretation:

1. Sit down, take a deep breath, and start focusing on the dream you want to interpret.
2. Let the thoughts about the dream and its elements come to the forefront of your mind. Pay attention to specific concepts, including the following:

    - What the dream tells you about how you appear to yourself and the role the experience could currently play in your life.
    - What the dream reveals about people in your life and how you react to their wants and needs.
    - What the dream tells you about the world around you based on how your environment appears in your dream.
    - What the dream suggests about the possible consequences of your actions. For example, if anything is forbidden in your dream, this could signify a penalty imposed by someone else or yourself in your waking life.

- Whether the dream implies inner conflict and a possible solution to resolving this discord.
3. Each of these concepts is linked to your behavior in your waking life. Analyzing them can help you create a map of your actions and understand why you do certain things. It enables you to follow your waking life actions through your dreams, anticipate consequences and other obstacles you may encounter, and predict how challenging it will be to reach your goals.
4. When you've finished analyzing your dreams and have drawn conclusions about your waking life experiences, try to organize your thoughts. You can do this by writing them down. Seeing them on paper may help you grasp their meaning better.

Intuitive and Reflective Approaches

Intuitive and reflective dream interpretation approaches involve techniques like dream journaling, free association, meditation, visualization, and other methods to deepen the connection with dream symbolism and facilitate interpretation.

Interpreting Your Dreams through Meditation

Meditation provides an excellent avenue for analyzing and interpreting difficult-to-understand dreams because it encourages you to reflect on them. During meditation, you observe and review recurring symbols and dream patterns. Taking time to reflect on the meanings of your dreams can help you understand them better.

Instructions:

1. Find a peaceful spot where you won't be disturbed. You'll need at least 20 minutes of quiet time.
2. Close your eyes and start breathing deeply until you reach a peaceful, meditative state. You'll know you're there when you feel your body and mind relaxed, and no more unwanted thoughts are popping up in your mind.
3. Recall the dream you want to interpret by bringing it close to your mind's eye. As you do, allow any insights to come to you without prejudice or bias. Don't try to control your thoughts. Let them pop up freely.

4. After observing the different parts of the dream, tap into your gut to see if there is anything else you need to know about the experience or any of its specific elements. Once again, allow whatever thought comes to arise on its own.
5. Reflect on whatever you learned from analyzing your dreams for as long as you feel necessary. When you're ready, take a deep breath and open your eyes.
6. If you wish, record what you've learned in a journal or on a voice recorder. You'll be able to review it later. You may find it easier to piece together the true meaning of your dream if you let some time pass after recalling it.

The Free-Association Method

Geared toward revealing the latent meaning of dreams, the free-association method is loosely based on Freud's dream theory. It's a relatively easy process as it only requires you to recall your dreams and express whatever comes to mind when you think of a specific dream.

Instructions:

1. Find a quiet space where you can relax. If you want to do the exercise by writing down your thoughts, take a pen and a piece of paper or your journal. If not, you can simply say the thoughts out loud.
2. Take a few moments to relax, then recall your dreams. Zero in on a few distinct elements of the image in your mind and pay attention to what ideas come to you.
3. Try to let the thoughts come without judgment. If the ideas seem too random, your mind may try to censor or dismiss them, but don't let it. Keep your focus sharp.
4. As you let the thoughts about your dream come freely, you'll start to understand repressed desires or conflicts you've put aside but which are still lingering in your subconscious.

Visualization

If you find expressing your thoughts about your dreams on paper or aloud uncomfortable, you might find it easier to visualize them instead. Visual guides are great aids for understanding complex concepts, including the meaning of your dreams.

Instructions:
1. Find a quiet and comfortable place where you can work without distractions.
2. Close your eyes, take a few deep breaths, and feel your body and mind relax.
3. When you're ready, start recalling your dream to interpret it.
4. You may find it easier to visualize and analyze specific scenes, a particular person or animal you saw in your dream, or a unique detail (like a color or symbol) that piqued your interest.
5. Bring whatever detail catches your attention in the dream as close as possible to your mind's eye. Look at them and try to understand what they're telling you. You may notice a certain sensation come over you as you observe the vision.
6. As you analyze the details one by one, you can see a connection between the different elements that weren't obvious when you were looking at the dream as a whole.
7. Visualizing and connecting the meanings of different dream elements will provide clarity and understanding of the hidden message behind the dream.

Analyzing Dreams via Journaling

Journaling is another way to enhance your intuition and, with it, the ability to understand the hidden messages of your dreams. Your intuition is the gateway to your subconscious, which is closely linked to dream recall and interpretation. In other words, it helps you translate experiences beyond your physical sense. Your gut feelings also enable you to interpret symbols through extrasensory perception by translating them into sensory experiences (what you experience through sounds, sights, smells, tastes, and feelings).

Instructions:
1. Schedule a specific time during the day to sit down and focus without distractions. This could be in the evening before going to sleep or in the morning right after waking up. Reflecting on why you want to record your dreams in a journal will help you focus on your goals of interpreting them.
2. Identify your specific intentions for dream journaling. For instance, for a more productive dream interpretation, you want to set an intention to connect with your intuition. Jot down your

intent in your journal and repeat this every time you make a new entry.

3. To boost your focus, take a few deep breaths to clear your mind of distractions. If you've finished dream journaling in the recent past, review the notes of your previous experiences and interpretations. This will help you remember crucial symbols and elements that appeared in your dreams. If doing this for the first time, proceed to the following step.

4. Start writing down your dream. Aim to record as many details as possible about your experience, including any emotions you experienced or vivid colors and notable symbols you saw in your dreams.

5. Some people find it easier to keep a structured entry of their dreams (including the date, experience, feelings, interpretations, and other details in a specific order). That said, you should write in a way that feels comfortable to you.

6. After recording them, take some time to reflect on what your dreams could signify to you personally. Consider how any detail you saw in your dream relates to your intuition. What is your gut telling you about them? Is there anything that makes you think of a waking-life situation or experience?

7. Note down any interpretations you make of your dreams or insights you gain from them. Even if the conclusion you've reached doesn't make sense at the moment, it may become clear later.

8. You can always return to analyzing journal entries to understand what your dreams are trying to communicate to you. As you do, you will notice patterns that can lead to more precise insights when interpreting a dream.

Chapter 7: How to Dream Recall

Forgetting your dreams is a normal human foible that is no cause for alarm. In fact, people dream around four to five times in one night, and if it so happens that you are unable to reconstruct your dreams when you wake up, that usually means your sleep wasn't disrupted.

For the longest time, experts believed that dreams only occurred during the REM stage of sleep (the periods in your sleep when rapid eye movement occurs along with a rapid heart rate and breathing without any signals being sent to the brain), which accounts for one-third of the sleep schedule. After further investigation, some evidence indicated that human dreams aren't exclusive to REM sleep but are distributed throughout the night. While dream and sleep research is usually a subject of controversy, some scientists believe that the dreams that occur during REM sleep are more story-oriented. The focus of REM sleep is to help you deal with emotional ordeals that may be too much to handle while you are awake. They also reached the conclusion that dreams that occur outside of REM are more thought-oriented, shorter, and harder to remember when you wake.

Whether or not you remember your dreams when you wake is not an indicator of the quality of sleep you get. Some people only remember their dreams because they wake up in the middle of them. With REM accounting for only around a quarter of a normal sleep schedule, you're looking at less than two hours of dreaming in which you may only end up remembering 10 minutes of it. On occasion, depending on the number of hours of sleep you get, REM sleep can occur more frequently and last longer.

The Science Behind Dream Recall

The human brain is divided into two parts: grey matter and white matter. Grey matter is associated with intellect and reasoning. White matter is concerned with dream recall.

To simplify the process, the two substances complement each other. How? Grey matter is responsible for processing the information within your brain, while white matter is more the liaison or the connector that links the different parts of the brain together, allowing information to flow.

Some researchers found that individuals with a higher ability to remember their dreams have more white matter residing in the medial prefrontal cortex, which is the part of your brain responsible for processing data about yourself.

Increased white matter in the brain may be responsible not only for better dream recall but also for creating dreams.

Why You Can't Remember Your Dreams

Humans' inability to remember their subconscious visions is a troubling topic for some people. And even though there is evidence that this phenomenon poses no threat to your physical or mental health, a lot of people have turned it into a quest that needs unearthing.

A more concerning challenge for others is that they tend to remember nightmares more than they do pleasant dreams. This is because nightmares jolt you out of sleep (REM state), which makes it easier to remember, and as you try to return to sleep, you usually, albeit unwillingly, end up thinking about it for a few minutes.

Pleasant dreams, unless they occur more than once, require more intentional attention and steps to commit the dream to memory.

So why can't everyone remember their dreams? There are a series of medical, social, and emotional reasons that can be listed to answer this question, including the following:

Anxiety: Dr. Shelby Harris, a behavioral sleep medicine specialist at the Albert Einstein College of Medicine in the Bronx, suggests that if you suffer from depression, anxiety, or high-stress levels, you're more likely to remember your dreams. However, that's not the healthiest way to do it because high-stress levels are more likely to cause you to wake up more often in the middle of your REM cycle, resulting in you remembering your trip down to your subconscious. This basically suggests that the lower the anxiety level, the lesser the chance of recall.

People with higher anxiety levels are more likely to recall their dreams.
https://unsplash.com/photos/rXrMv7mXUEs?utm_source=unsplash&utm_medium=referral&utm_content=creditShareLink

Physiological Differences and Personality

In some studies, it was concluded that teenage females had a higher chance of remembering their dreams than males. This study unearthed a link between recalling dreams and being creative. Participants who viewed themselves as creative found it easier to remember their dreams than others who didn't identify as such.

Other studies found that age is a contributor as well, with young men remembering their dreams more often than older ones. People living in cities and urban districts can also dream recall better than people in rural areas, though that may be due to the fact that the noise associated with the living conditions causes them to wake up more during REM cycles.

Medication and Medical issues

Some research points out that medications that treat depression may be a cause for suppressing dream sleep. Sleep Apnea, which is a condition that causes pauses in breathing during sleep, has also been accused of affecting the amount of time people spend dreaming.

Benefits of Dream Recall

Salvador Dali, whose paintings were inspired by his dreams, and Dimitri Mendeleev, who saw the periodic table in his unconscious state, are evidence of the importance of dream recall. Dreams foster ideas and creativity and allow for better problem-solving techniques.

Identifying Dream Patterns

As you document your dreams over an extended period of time, patterns start to emerge. Repeated dreams can reveal intimate details about your waking existence that you may have missed before. As you get more accustomed to the patterns, you can reach a level of controlling your dreams while unconscious. This ability can help you understand how your subconscious mind functions and the symbols in each dream.

Cataloging Your Memories

Consolidating your memories is the key role of dreams. The events you go through during your days and in previous weeks are usually embedded into your dreams. As that happens, your memory improves, and your dream recall ability is heightened. Dreams help solidify the memories in your long-term memory bank and eliminate trivial and unnecessary ones.

Improves Creativity

Some researchers share the belief that dreams help mental breakthroughs that cannot be achieved during waking hours. Dreams help address issues and unusual events that occur during the day that you may not necessarily have noticed. They believe this is due to the strange and unusual structure of dreams and the different kinds of thinking required for dreaming instead of using the logical brain when you're awake.

Processing Emotions

A common topic usually associated with dreams is emotions that are suppressed or ignored during your waking hours and usually make an appearance during your slumber.

Dreams are integral to putting you in challenging situations you are less likely to encounter in real life. Nightmare scenarios can help the sleeper adapt to difficult real-life situations, almost like a simulation of danger and how you could react to it. Your reactions to scary or embarrassing situations in your dreams can dictate or improve your responses while you are awake.

Lucid Dreaming

Lucid dreaming is the phenomenon of being aware that you're asleep and dreaming. You are observing the events of your dream with the knowledge that they are not real. On some occasions, you may be able to change the course of the dream as it unfolds.

Though lucid dreaming comes spontaneously to some people, others practice methods to improve their ability and the frequency of lucid dreaming.

As you remember more of your dreams, you get better at understanding and translating their meaning and purpose. Consequently, this leads to controlling the dreams you have. The more you document your dreams, the higher the likelihood of remembering them and being more aware when they occur.

Methods to Improve Dream Recall

Is remembering your dreams something you can practice and improve? Yes.

Dr. Jade Wu, a clinical Psychologist, believes that setting the intention to remember the dream in the morning is the first step toward dream recall.

A method Dr. Wu recommends is simply repeating to yourself a mantra along the lines of "I will remember my dream in the morning" before going to bed, starting your brain engine working in the right direction. The same mentality can be applied to nightmares. If you address a bad dream during your waking hours by changing its script and rehearsing it several times, say for twenty minutes a day, you're conditioning your brain to experience a different ending as you sleep.

There is more than one technique that can be implemented by those who wish to recall and commit their dreams to their long-term memories, such as the following:

Keeping a Dream Journal

Journals are a widely recommended method when it comes to exploring your emotions and mental state. With dreams, a journal acts as a jigsaw puzzle as it helps you put together the different pieces of the dreams as you continue to remember them during the day.

Keep a notepad and pen next to your bed, and as you rise from your slumber, write down all you can remember from your unconscious encounters. The writing doesn't have to be in order, nor do you need to create a cohesive story. Small cues and phrases about what you experienced will jump-start your memory later on to remember more details.

Some researchers recommend that you keep your eyes closed as you wake so that the details are clearer in your head. Doing this helps to avoid being distracted by your room and surroundings, which may cause you to forget bits of the dream.

Try to continue recording any fragments you remember throughout the day. Sometimes, a word, situation, or object can jolt your memory into remembering fragments of the dreams as the day goes on.

Realistically, you won't always remember your dreams or succeed in jotting them down quickly enough. However, persistence is key. The more you try to remember and the more you practice, the easier it gets.

Set the Intention to Remember

Your mind believes the thoughts you feed it. As previously suggested by Dr. Wu, try to make a mental resolution before you go to bed so that you'll remember your dreams.

It usually takes a few tries before it works, but the more you do it, the more your brain will divert more effort toward what you're trying to achieve. With time, you'll find it easier to think clearly in the morning about your dreams.

This is quite similar to what's known as the law of attraction. What you send out into the world will come back to you. What you tell your mind will eventually apply.

Set a Comfortable and Consistent Sleep Schedule

Back to basics! Your body's natural sleeping hours are at night. The preferred and recommended time for sleep is at night when you feel tired and wake up early, around eight or nine a.m.

This means refraining from staying up late until two or three in the morning. When this happens, the biological clock is forced to extend your sleep schedule, leading to extra sleeping hours in the morning, which disrupts the body's chemistry.

A good night's sleep improves your overall health and brain function, not to mention your mood.

Evening sleep tends to release specific hormones linked to darkness, such as melatonin, cortisol, growth hormone, and many others. These hormones are essential for circadian regulation and glucose and lipid homeostasis.

When your sleep schedule is irregular, it affects your ability to recall your dreams because your focus will be poor. Sleep disturbances also impact healing and conditions such as obesity, insulin insensitivity, and diabetes.

Bad quality sleep means less opportunity for quality **REM** sleep, which is when dreams frequently occur, and means that not only will you be tired, but you won't be able to remember your dreams either.

Try, to the best of your ability, to keep your sleep environment free of noise, lights, or any distractions that may disrupt your sleep.

Implementing a power-down hour before sleep makes it easier to maintain your sleep schedule. Avoid any stressful triggers, screens, food, or loud noises. Dim the lights in the room and try to engage in relaxing exercises such as reading, which helps take your mind off daily stresses. Ensure you're hydrated and water is within arm's reach by your bed.

Try Something New

Break away from your regular routine every day. Every time you do something new, exciting, or unusual, chances are your brain will save them in your memory, and the probability of having interesting dreams increases.

Set the Mood before Bed

You can follow some recommended techniques during the "Power Down Hour" that can induce more restful sleep.

Start winding down by calming your mind. A calm and peaceful mood makes you less likely to experience nightmares and increases the chances you'll remember your dreams.

You can do that in numerous ways:

Meditation

Meditations and deep breathing exercises before bed calm the nervous system. You don't need to spend an hour on them; 10 minutes each day before bed should suffice.

Warm Bath
Fill your bathtub with warm water and add a few drops of essential oil to relax the muscles and wind down.

Reading a Book
Reading a book has a way of taking your mind away from the realities of your daily anxieties and relaxing your brain.

Artwork
Try drawing, doodling, or coloring in an adult coloring book. These exercises are perfect for clearing the mind and helping you focus on the activity rather than the thoughts in your head.

Consider What You Want to Dream About
Take a moment to think about what kind of experience you want to have during your sleep and try to visualize and manifest it.

Lights Out
Turn off or dim the lights an hour before bed to induce sleepiness. The better the quality of the sleep, the higher the chance of better dream recall.

Avoid Alcohol and Chemicals
Try to refrain from using alcoholic beverages, medications, and food at least three hours before you go to bed.

The chemicals included in these items can have negative effects on your nervous system and can impact your ability to remember your dreams as well as lower the quality of your sleep.

Wake Up Naturally
Try not to set an alarm, but wake up slowly and naturally instead. Try to linger just a few minutes more in the half-sleepy state when you wake up. Avoid jumping out of bed immediately. If you need to set the alarm, make sure it's within reach so you don't move too much to silence it, and set it to a calming sound rather than radio or loud noises.

As you wake up, try setting your eyes on a singular object rather than moving your gaze around the room. Stay focused on the object until you remember the dream, and it's registered to memory.

Use Supplements
Some people may find some of the previous exercises tedious and hard to follow. If you're one of them, there are other natural ingredients you can try to induce dream recall.

Aromatherapy is a proven memory and nervous booster, specifically if you use rosemary essential oil. Sprinkling a couple of drops on your pillow before bed should do the trick.

It has been suggested that drinking Mugwort tea is a way to make your dreams more vivid and lifelike. Consequently, this makes them easier to remember.

Increasing amino acids in your diet can also help improve memory, cognition, and the perception of happiness.

Dream Incubation

Dream incubation is the practice of trying to specify what you dream about. To purposefully decide what your dream will be before falling asleep and set the appropriate environment to nurture the required result.

This method is often used if you are trying to solve a problem and shouldn't be confused with lucid dreaming. While lucid dreaming involves the knowledge that you are dreaming mixed with control over the dream, dream incubation is about influencing the dream before it occurs and during your sleep.

This method helps the dreamer to use the subconscious to solve a problem their conscious mind is battling.

Here are a few simple steps to start you up with the practice:

- As you get ready for bed, visualize the problem clearly in your mind. Set a clear intention for the dream and the direction you need it to take. If you're having trouble doing it mentally, use a pen and paper, write down the intention and problem, and review it before bed. You can start this process early on in the day. It doesn't have to be right before your scheduled sleep time.

- Limit screen time before bed and try to relax as best you can. Try visualizing the dream. You can use little triggers like a picture if there is someone specific you wish to dream of.

- Keep a pen and paper handy next to your bed before drifting off to sleep.

- As you wake up, stay still and don't get out of bed right away. See if you can recall your dream and write it down. Document everything you remember, even the emotions you felt during the dream.

- Don't lose patience. With dream incubation, practice makes perfect. Keep in mind that as you start practicing incubation, there may be some resistance from your subconscious. If your subconscious deems the intention of the dream insignificant, it will leave signals for you within the dream.

Chapter 8: Identifying Patterns in Dreams

A deeper understanding of your subconscious will be the key to decoding your dreams and identifying any recurring patterns. This pattern identification can provide profound insights that enable an individual to understand and control their dream realm better. Most lucid dreams are vivid and include a plethora of elements - people, places, events, and emotions presented as a multi-colored tapestry. The dream may seem like a mess, but when you start recognizing the patterns, everything falls into place.

Similarly, seeing repeated environments, symbols, emotions, and scenarios in dreams is associated with inner goals, conflicts, and aspirations. Recognizing these elements and understanding their meaning is an opportunity for introspection and self-exploration. These repetitive elements can be interpreted to understand their purpose and address unresolved desires, emotions, and conflicts.

Several techniques are used to identify and comprehend these patterns. One popular approach is to keep a dream journal where you can record the events occurring in the dream and use the information as a reference point for comparison and analysis. This comparison will let you identify recurring elements you must recognize and address. These frequent thoughts and patterns point toward issues in real life and indicate that they need to address these issues in their waking lives.

Recognizing these patterns can be confusing, so seeking guidance from a dream analyst can help you figure out the meaning behind these patterns. Therapists are trained specifically to help you interpret dreams from a psychological perspective and boost self-awareness and personal growth.

Identifying and understanding repeated dream elements uncovers more about your inner self, letting you see the hidden aspects of your subconscious mind. Staying curious and open-minded is essential to develop a more profound understanding of dream patterns and their links to your inner self.

Getting Familiar with Recurring Dream Elements

Understanding common signs, environments, and scenarios makes knowing the associated meaning and symbolism easier. Each element you see in a dream realm will have a different interpretation in different scenarios. A single symbol can have multiple meanings, depending on the environment and relevant details. According to psychologists, the subconscious mind frequently uses objects, characters, people, and places to represent complex emotions that are challenging to face or express in waking life.

An element's dream interpretation and meaning can also change with the person. For example, a person sees their home in a dream. Generally, it symbolizes security and stability but can evoke childhood memories and upbringing for another person. Carl Jung, a renowned psychologist and dream interpreter, emphasizes that becoming familiar with archetypal symbols is necessary. These symbols carry a universal meaning and are commonly represented in lucid dreams. Some examples include the sun, which is linked to vitality and life, the moon, which symbolizes emotions, and traveling in a lucid dream, which translates to transformation and growth.

Although these archetype symbols have an ordinary meaning, cultural influences, and regional beliefs can still influence their meanings. For example, a person from a coastal area may associate the ocean with positive emotions. In contrast, others who have had a traumatic experience while traveling by sea will see the ocean dream as emotionally distressing and may interpret it differently.

Understanding the context of the dream and then interpreting the symbols will lead to accurate interpretation. It's not a single event, character, or object that will define the overall message. Instead, a collective of every element in the lucid dream will determine the true meaning of the dream. In a nutshell, if you want to understand what your subconscious is trying to express, understanding common symbols and related elements will help. Furthermore, don't forget to analyze the dream from a cultural and spiritual perspective as well to get the whole picture. Lastly, keep an open mind and be willing to learn to achieve the best outcomes.

Common Patterns and Symbols of the Dream World

Recurring Elements

These elements can be anything from an object, place, or person. They often have symbolic significance and are seen as a vital message from the subconscious due to their repetitiveness in dreams.

Here's an example to help you develop a better understanding. Imagine a dreamer frequently dreaming about a tree producing red apples in most of their dreams. The red apple tree in the dream world is associated with fertility, life, and growth but can have several other meanings. The tree can symbolize passion, love, aspirations, or even anger in specific scenarios. In another scenario where a person is emotionally neglected in waking life, seeing the same red apple tree signifies the need for self-care to improve emotional and physical well-being.

Recurring Themes

Sometimes, the subconscious mind or events in the real world influence lucid dreams, resulting in recurring themes, scenarios, and dream experiences. These repeated scenarios point to the concerns of the dreamer's subconscious emotions and conflicting issues that they still carry within their mind.

When people face insecurity in relationships or don't have set goals and aspirations, they could see themselves having dreams of being in unfamiliar locations. This scenario indicates the dreamer's confusion about life matters. This scenario can also show the dreamer's fear of making the wrong choices or feeling disconnected from their life's purpose. As the dreamer explores this recurring theme and understands its meaning, they may gain awareness of their internal struggles and be motivated to seek guidance, find clarity, and regain a sense of purpose in their waking lives.

Recurring Symbols

Recurring symbols in dreams are abstract representations that consistently appear across various experiences. These symbols can carry universal or personal meanings, requiring interpretation based on the dreamer's unique experiences and associations.

Consider a dreamer who frequently encounters a white dove in their dreams. The white dove is a widely recognized symbol of peace and spirituality. However, the symbol may hold more profound personal significance for this particular dreamer. The recurring appearance of the white dove might indicate the dreamer's subconscious desire for inner peace and harmony. Alternatively, it could symbolize their longing for resolution in a specific conflict or difficult situation. In this case, the white dove is a powerful and recurring symbol that reflects the dreamer's quest for tranquility and a peaceful resolution in their waking life.

Recurring Experiences

Recurring experiences in dreams are specific events that happen repeatedly, such as flying, falling, or being chased. These experiences often carry emotional weight and may offer insights into the dreamer's waking life struggles or aspirations.

Imagine a dreamer who frequently dreams of flying gracefully through the sky. This experience could signify the dreamer's freedom, liberation, and desire to rise above challenges and limitations. It also indicates a sense of empowerment and confidence in the dreamer's waking life. On the other hand, a different dreamer may frequently dream of falling from great heights. This recurring experience could reflect the dreamer's fear of failure, a lack of control, or feelings of vulnerability. By exploring these frequent experiences, the dreamer can gain a better understanding of their subconscious fears and aspirations.

Sequential Dreams

Sequential dreams occur when there is a continuity of events or a developing storyline across multiple dream sessions. These dreams may suggest a deeper exploration of the dreamer's psyche or an ongoing emotional process.

Consider a dreamer who experiences a series of dreams involving a mysterious quest. In the first dream, the dreamer embarks on a journey to find a hidden treasure, but the dream ends before they reach their goal. In the subsequent dreams, the dreamer faces challenges and encounters different characters, each providing clues to the treasure's location. As the dreamer continues this dream series, they metaphorically navigate through their subconscious, seeking answers to unresolved questions and gaining insights into their psyche. The sequential dreams represent a continuing emotional journey, and the dreamer's progress in the dream world reflects their evolving self-discovery and personal growth in waking life.

Lucid Dreams

Lucid dreams are dreams in which the dreamer becomes aware that they are dreaming and may have some control over the dream narrative. Lucid dreaming offers a unique opportunity for conscious exploration of the dream world.

A person experiences lucid dreams frequently, allowing them to recognize when they are dreaming and actively engage with their dreams. In a lucid dream, the dreamer may fly, explore fantastical landscapes, or confront their fears head-on. These lucid dream experiences indicate high self-awareness and control over one's subconscious mind. For this dreamer, these dreams could serve as a platform for creative expression, problem-solving, or emotional catharsis. The ability to lucid dream can be a powerful tool for self-exploration and personal development, as the dreamer gains conscious access to their inner thoughts, emotions, and desires, ultimately leading to greater self-understanding and empowerment.

Recurring Colors

Recurring colors in dreams can hold symbolic meanings and emotional associations, providing insights into the dreamer's psychological state and experiences.

A dreamer may frequently dream of the color blue. The color blue often symbolizes calmness, tranquility, and emotional stability. In the dreamer's case, this recurring color could indicate a longing for emotional peace and a desire to find a sense of calm amidst life's challenges. Alternatively, it could represent the dreamer's reflective nature and inclination to explore their emotions and inner world. The recurring appearance of blue may prompt the dreamer to examine their emotional well-being and seek opportunities for self-care and inner harmony.

Recurring Numbers

Numbers that repeat in dreams may carry numerological significance or represent essential aspects of the dreamer's life.

For example, a person consistently dreams of the number three. The number three is often associated with creativity, unity, and completion. In this dreamer's recurring dreams, number three might symbolize the dreamer's desire for creative expression and a sense of wholeness in their life. It could also signify a need for integration of balance, mind, body, and spirit. By paying attention to the recurrence of the number, the dreamer can explore their creative potential and seek opportunities for personal growth and fulfillment in various areas of their life.

Understanding these patterns in dreams requires attentive observation, self-reflection, and exploring personal experiences, emotions, and associations. Keeping a dream journal and discussing patterns with a therapist or dream analyst leads to deeper insights into the subconscious mind. It is essential to remember that dream interpretation is highly subjective, and the significance may vary significantly from one individual to another. By approaching dream analysis with an open mind and a willingness to explore the depths of the subconscious, dreamers can gain profound insights into their inner selves and unlock the potential for personal transformation and self-discovery.

Techniques to Identify Dream Patterns

Dreams have always been a source of fascination and mystery, offering a window into the inner workings of the subconscious mind. People often encounter patterns within dreams, such as specific elements, themes, or symbols that frequently appear across different experiences. These recurring patterns can have significant meanings, reflecting your deepest emotions, desires, and unresolved conflicts. By identifying and understanding them, you learn a lot about your psyche, fostering self-awareness, personal growth, and a deeper understanding of yourself. This comprehensive guide will explore step-by-step techniques to help you identify, analyze, and interpret recurring dream patterns, unlocking hidden messages from your subconscious mind.

1. Keep a Dream Journal

Begin by establishing a dedicated dream journal that you keep beside your bed. When you wake up, take a few moments to jot down all the details you can remember from your dream. Include elements, themes, symbols, emotions, and relevant experiences.

- Place a dedicated notebook and pen beside your bed.
- As soon as you wake up, before getting out of bed or engaging in other activities, take a moment to recall your dream.
- Write down all the details you can remember, including elements, themes, symbols, emotions, and significant experiences from the dream.
- Remember to record your dreams in your journal regularly, even if you can only remember fragments at first.

2. Identify Recurring Elements

Regularly review your dream journal and identify any recurring elements that appear across multiple dream experiences. These could be specific objects, people, places, or symbols that consistently manifest in your dreams.

3. Reflect on Personal Associations

For each recurring element, take time to reflect on your associations and emotions related to it. Consider how these elements connect to your waking experiences, memories, and feelings. Be open to any intuitive insights that arise during this reflection process.

- Take time to reflect on each recurring element and consider your associations and emotions related to them.
- Ask yourself why these elements hold significance for you and how they connect to your waking life experiences or memories.

4. Analyze Dream Themes

Identify and analyze recurring themes or scenarios that unfold in your dreams. Look for everyday situations or emotions that seem to repeat themselves, regardless of the specific elements involved.

- Look for recurring themes or scenarios that unfold in your dreams. Identify everyday situations, emotions, or challenges that repeat across different dreams.

- Pay attention to emerging patterns, such as dreams involving relationships, work, or specific settings.

5. Explore Emotional Content

Delve into the emotional content of your dreams. Take note of any strong emotions, fears, or unresolved feelings that appear consistently in your dream narratives. Emotional patterns are valuable clues about your inner psyche.

- Examine the emotional content of your dreams, taking note of any intense emotions, fears, or unresolved feelings that consistently appear.
- Consider how these emotions may relate to your waking life and the events or situations that trigger similar feelings.

6. Consider the Dream Context

Examine the context in which recurring elements or themes occur. Pay attention to the setting, other characters, and events surrounding the repeating patterns. Understanding the broader context can provide additional context for interpreting dream patterns.

- Analyze the context in which recurring elements or themes occur. Look at the setting, other characters, and events surrounding the repeating patterns.
- Consider how these contextual details might provide additional insights into the meaning of the dream patterns.

7. Seek Professional Guidance

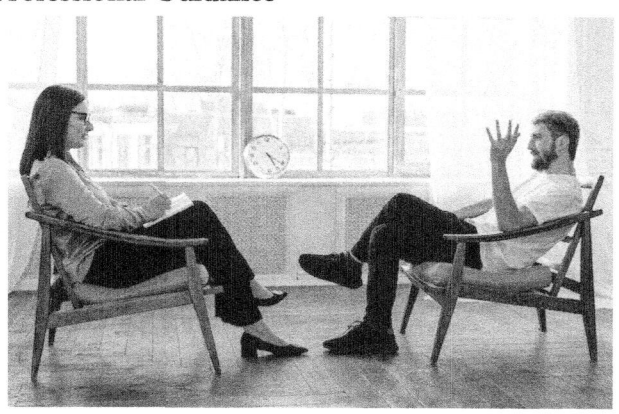

Therapists can offer alternative perspectives on the meanings of your dreams.
https://www.pexels.com/photo/person-in-black-pants-and-black-shoes-sitting-on-brown-wooden-chair-4101143/

If a specific dream pattern remains unclear or evokes intense emotions, consider seeking guidance from a therapist or dream analyst who has expertise in dream interpretation. They can offer valuable knowledge and alternative perspectives.

8. Engage in Active Imagination

To further explore the meaning of dream elements and symbols, engage in active imagination or free association. Allow your mind to wander and write down any thoughts, images, or memories that come to mind when you're contemplating the recurring patterns.

9. Connect with Your Intuition

Trust your intuition and inner wisdom when exploring dream patterns. Often, the subconscious communicates through subtle feelings and intuitive insights. Stay open to the guidance that arises from within.

10. Practice Mindfulness

Practice mindfulness and meditation to become more aware of your thoughts and emotions throughout the day. Mindfulness can help you notice patterns and connections between your waking life and dream experiences.

11. Analyze Sequential Dreams

If you experience sequential dreams, analyze the progression and connections between different dream episodes. Look for common themes or lessons that emerge from the series of dreams. Sequential dreams may offer a deeper exploration of specific themes or personal growth over time.

12. Engage in Dream Incubation

Before going to sleep, intend to explore a specific dream pattern or question in your dreams. This technique, known as dream incubation, can clarify recurring themes and facilitate personal growth.

13. Embrace Symbol Dictionaries and Resources

Consult books, online resources, or symbol dictionaries exploring meanings of common dream symbols. However, remember that personal associations with symbols are essential for accurate interpretation.

14. Practice Lucid Dreaming

Explore lucid dreaming techniques to become consciously aware and control your dreams. Lucid dreaming allows you to engage with recurring patterns actively and explore their significance.

By using these step-by-step techniques and remaining patient and open-minded, you can start a profound journey of self-exploration through your dreams. Identifying and understanding recurring dream patterns offers transformative insights into your subconscious mind, fosters personal growth, and facilitates a deeper connection with your inner self. As you venture into the depths of your dreams, remember that dream interpretation is highly subjective, and the significance of recurring patterns may vary significantly from one individual to another. Embrace this exploration with curiosity and an open heart, and allow your dreams to guide your path of self-discovery.

Chapter 9: Lucid Dreaming Techniques

When a person is in a dream state, they don't realize the dream may not be real. However, some people become fully aware they are dreaming and know that none of it is real. Lucid dreaming is a dream state where you are fully conscious and understand that you are inside a dream. Unlike regular dreams, it's like waking up inside your imagination, where you are somewhat in control.

Imagine you're in a dream, walking past a beautiful meadow, and suddenly, you see a unicorn fly by. At this moment, you realize that your world is a creation of your mind. This realization of being in a dream state while fully aware is termed lucid dreaming.

Once you know you're dreaming, you can start doing some awesome things like:

Take Control

When lucid dreaming, changing the dream's scenery and environment is not a big deal. People with years of practice can make things appear out of thin air and even shapeshift into animals or objects from their imagination.

Sharpen Your Senses

You may feel more aware and conscious during a lucid dream than in the real world. The senses are in overdrive, and everything will appear vivid, intense, and realistic.

Be the Boss

During a lucid dream, it's possible to let events unfold naturally or to take the driving seat and ride on your way. You can be an active stakeholder in the dream, making impactful choices and determining the chain of events that follows.

Beat Bad Vibes

Understanding your mind and mastering lucid dreaming techniques is handy for dealing with nightmares. When you know that you are dreaming, facing fears head-on becomes easier. You can transform the scary monsters trying to haunt you into harmless butterflies or sheep.

Unlock Your Mind

Mastering the lucid dreaming technique is like opening a gateway into your subconsciousness. With increasing experience, you can use lucid dreaming to troubleshoot inner thoughts that are bugging you and explore thoughts buried deep within the mind.

While some people can have lucid dreaming experiences without a hitch, others may need to use certain techniques to make it happen. These include reality checks, journaling, and meditation. The lucid dreaming experience will eventually change from person to person, and the control each person has in their dreams also varies.

The Difference between Regular and Lucid Dreaming

Awareness

You are unaware of being in a dream state in a regular dream. The experience feels legitimate, triggering many emotions and making you go with the flow without questioning the authenticity of the events. In contrast, lucid dreaming is a state of dream where you become aware that you are in a dream and that the events you are witnessing are a creation of your mind.

Control

The events unfolding in a regular dream are not controllable. You'll find you are more likely an observer in most regular dreams, but in a lucid dreaming state, it's possible to take control and influence the dream. Manipulating the environment, changing the course of events, and making a decision are possible in a lucid dreaming state.

Realization of Impossibility

While experiencing dreams, things can get quite creative as it's possible in that dream for you to fly in the sky or meet mythical creatures from ancient folklore. Having these experiences may not feel like a big deal in regular dreams, but when lucid dreaming, you'll instantly notice the events unfolding in front of your eyes from the dream world – events that are impossible in real life. For example, talking to a deceased person close to your heart can make you realize it's a dream.

Emotional Involvement

When in a regular dream, you'll feel a surge of emotions, but the type of emotions will be unpredictable. You'll be a passive participant in a regular dream. Evoking powerful emotions is possible in a lucid dream. Having control of the dream world can make it easier to revamp the emotional experience.

Memory Recall

Remembering what happened in a regular dream is more challenging than a lucid dream. You might struggle a lot and only remember scarce details after waking up. However, in a lucid dream state, you can remember everything in great detail due to heightened self-awareness. The details can even be recalled several days after the experience.

Although experiencing lucid dreaming is natural and unintentional, there are several techniques people have mastered to induce it during their sleep. For most people, tapping into the dream world is to open new paths toward personal growth, explore the inner self, resolve internal conflicts, or let their imagination run wild and enhance creativity.

Is Lucid Dreaming Similar to Out-of-Body Experiences (OBE)?

Although there are several similarities, both phenomena are distinct due to the following aspects.

Nature of Experience

In a lucid dream, the dreamer is already aware that they are dreaming and that the events unfolding are their mind's creation. They understand that the events are not actual and may even gain control to manipulate dreams. In contrast, the OBE experience is a sensation where a person feels detached from their physical body. It's like the spirit leaves the body while visually seeing the spirit move outside the body.

Location of Awareness

During a lucid dream, the person experiencing the dream is engaged mentally with the dream environment. They are aware of the dream state and have their self-consciousness intact. However, in an OBE, the individual will feel their spirit move out of the physical body alongside their self-consciousness and control over the physical body.

Perception of the Physical World

The lucid dream experience is surreal, where many events can be inconsistent with physical reality. The dreamer will control the dream environment and its elements while knowing it's not real. However, in out-of-body experiences, the environment they interact with is similar to the real world. The experience is like seeing an object or a real-world event unfold that the person may not have known if not in the OBE state.

Occurrence and Triggers

While both lucid dreaming and OBEs occur naturally and can be triggered by practicing several techniques, the methods used to trigger each experience differ. People practice techniques like reality checks, meditation, lucid dreaming exercises, and similar methods to induce lucid dreaming. On the other hand, OBEs are triggered through intense meditation practices, exposure to extreme physical or emotional events, sleep paralysis, and near-death experiences.

OBEs and lucid dreaming are unique gateways to an altered state of consciousness that offer to explore insights from the human mind.

While lucid dreaming and OBEs are different experiences, they offer unique insights into altered states of consciousness and the remarkable capabilities of the human mind. Both phenomena have been subjects of interest and exploration by individuals, researchers, and spiritual practitioners for many years.

Potential Benefits of Lucid Dreaming

Self-Awareness

Out of the many potential benefits, self-awareness improves with lucid dreaming. The experience allows individuals to recognize their subconscious thoughts, understand inner emotions better, and explore different emotions while staying within their dreams. This enhanced self-awareness can promote introspection that can extend to waking life.

Creativity

It's like a playground for creativity where you or the individual who adopts lucid dreaming techniques can let their creativity paint the dream canvas. Dreamers in lucid dreaming can manipulate environments to their will, promoting imaginative experiences. Practicing this creativity in the dream world influences artistic endeavors and boosts real-life innovative thinking abilities.

Overcoming Nightmares

Learning to induce lucid dreaming is beneficial for people who have frequent nightmares. When used effectively, this powerful tool can help overcome fears and increase the courage needed to deal with these nightmares. For example, if you are facing issues related to nightmares, learning to induce a lucid dream state and facing the demons haunting you'll become easier. When you already know that you are in a dream state and can manipulate the surroundings to your liking, confronting your demons and transforming these negative scenarios into positive experiences will be much easier.

Skill Enhancement

Dream experts and research on lucid dreaming revealed that practicing several skills within the dream world can significantly boost that specific skill in the real world. Avid lucid dreaming practitioners see the lucid dream state as a mental training ground where creative people, like musicians and artists, can enhance their creativity without restriction.

Stress Reduction

Lucid dreaming can help reduce stress.
https://www.pexels.com/photo/woman-sitting-by-lake-185939/

Lucid dreams are also an escape from the stresses and problems associated with life. Being in control and shaping the dream experience to create a calming effect can significantly decrease stress levels. Besides stress reduction, your mood improves as well.

Emotional Healing

Lucid dreaming provides a safe space for processing and healing emotional issues. People may use lucid dreams to confront past traumas, resolve conflicts, or gain insights into their emotional well-being.

Personal Development

The self-reflective nature of lucid dreaming can lead to personal growth and a deeper understanding of thoughts, beliefs, and aspirations. It can be a valuable tool for introspection and self-improvement.

Spiritual Exploration

For some people, lucid dreaming offers opportunities for spiritual exploration and mystical experiences. People use lucid dreams to connect with their spiritual beliefs, encounter spiritual figures, or explore higher states of consciousness.

Fun and Adventure

Besides the more profound benefits, lucid dreaming is a source of enjoyment and excitement. Lucid dreamers can have incredible adventures, explore new worlds, and engage in activities that may not be possible in waking life.

Techniques to Induce Lucid Dreaming

Reality Checks

It seems like a simple technique, but it can do wonders when you get the hang of it. All you need to do is perform a reality check at fixed intervals. The chances of completing a reality check within the dream state increase when you persistently practice it during waking hours. The goal is to notice any discrepancies or surreal events that indicate the dream state. Here are a few commonly used reality-check techniques:

Pushing Finger through the Palm

Place a finger on the opposite palm and push the finger. In the dream world, the finger can pass through, whereas, in reality, it won't. You can also try pressing the finger through a nearby object for a similar reality check.

Focusing on an Object

You can look at the clock, read a book, or focus on a stationary object for a while, then look away and again look back at the object. If everything remains the same, it's the real world, but when it's the dream world, the object can be seen distorted.

Practicing these checks trains the brain to question and identify the current state of consciousness. The chances of recognizing that you are in a dream state will slowly increase when you persistently perform these reality checks.

Dream Journaling

Keep a notebook and a pen nearby when sleeping, and try writing it down as soon as you wake up. Recalling the events and writing them down will boost your dream-recalling abilities. The more you remember what happened in the dream world, the more you can understand the dream environment, locations, patterns, and recurring dream signs.

Mnemonic Induction of Lucid Dreams (MILD)

This technique involves setting a solid intention to induce a lucid dream when in a deep sleep state. Repeat a phrase or affirmation like "I will have a lucid dream tonight" while imagining yourself taking control of the dream world. You should focus on feelings of power and understand you can be aware even in a dream state. Mastering the technique will require practice and persistence, but the hard work will pay off, creating a solid connection between your real-life brain and the dream mind.

Wake-Back-to-Bed (WBTB)

The technique requires the dreamer to wake up after four to six hours of sleep. Under ideal circumstances where you have a great sleep routine, you'll go to bed early. Waking up after the specified period is crucial because most lucid dreams occur during **REM** sleep. Waking up just before the **REM** sleep time frame and sleeping again can do the trick. Doing activities for wakeful awareness, reading about lucid dreaming, and meditation are some tools for better control over your sleep routine. The focus here is to sleep again after making yourself more alert.

Wake-Initiated Lucid Dream (WILD)

The **WILD** technique involves entering a lucid dream directly from a waking state while maintaining awareness. It requires a high level of mental focus and relaxation. As you lie down to sleep, focus on the hypnagogic imagery that appears during the transition from wakefulness to sleep. These are the visual and auditory sensations you experience as you drift off to sleep. Stay mentally alert and observe these sensations without reacting to them. As you do this, the dream may form around you, and you can "step" into the dream while being aware. This technique is more advanced and may require practice to achieve success.

Meditation and Mindfulness

Meditation can improve your self-awareness.
https://www.pexels.com/photo/woman-meditating-in-the-outdoors-2908175/

Practicing meditation and mindfulness during your waking hours can improve your self-awareness and ability to stay present in the moment. Carry this mindfulness into your dream state by reminding yourself to stay aware and present as you dream. This helps you to recognize when you are in a dream and achieve lucidity.

Wake Up Naturally

If you wake up naturally during the night without using an alarm, use this as an opportunity to attempt lucid dreaming. While lying in bed, keep your mind focused on the idea of having a lucid dream as you fall back to sleep. Since you are already in partial wakefulness, you may find it easier to become lucid when you re-enter the dream state.

External Cues

Some lucid dreamers use external cues to bring about lucidity within their dreams. These cues can be flashing lights, sounds, or vibrations set up strategically in their sleeping environment. The idea is that these cues catch their attention while dreaming, reminding them to question their reality and realize they are dreaming.

Reality Testing

- **Choose Reality Check Cues:** Select two to three reality check cues that are easy to perform and remember. For example, you can push your finger through your palm, check the time on a clock, or read a text.
- **Set Intention and Reminder:** Throughout the day, set a clear intention to perform reality checks regularly. You can set alarms or use daily routines (e.g., every time you pass through a door or see a specific object) as reminders to do the checks.
- **Perform Reality Checks Mindfully:** When the reminder comes, pause and perform the reality check mindfully. Don't just go through the motions. Truly question your consciousness and wonder if you're in a dream.
- **Question the Results:** When you perform a reality check, don't assume you're awake because it matches reality. Instead, genuinely question the results, even in waking life. This habit will carry over into your dreams, making it more likely you'll be able to examine your dream state.
- **Make It a Habit:** Be consistent with reality testing, even if you haven't yet experienced a lucid dream. Making it a daily habit will reinforce the behavior and increase the likelihood of doing reality checks in your dreams.

Dream Journaling

- **Keep the Journal Close:** Place a notebook and pen (or a smartphone) near your bed to ensure it is readily available when you wake up.
- **Write Immediately Upon Waking:** As soon as you wake up, focus on recalling your dreams. Even if you only remember fragments, jot them down in your journal. Write in the present tense to make the memories more vivid.
- **Capture Sensory Details:** Include as many sensory details as possible in your dream journaling. Describe the sights, sounds, feelings, and emotions you experienced during the dream.

- **Identify Dream Signs:** Look for recurring themes, people, places, or events in your dreams. These are called dream signs and can be helpful cues for recognizing dreams in the future.
- **Review and Reflect:** Take time to read your dream journal regularly. Look for patterns or common dream signs. Reflect on your dreams and ask yourself if anything seemed unusual or if any moments could have triggered lucidity.
- **Set Intentions Before Sleep:** Before going to bed each night, set a positive intention to remember and become more aware of your dream experiences. This intention can enhance dream recall and awareness during dreaming.
- **Be Patient:** Dream recall and lucid dreaming may not happen immediately. Be patient and persistent with dream journaling, as it's essential to becoming more aware of your dreams.

Combining reality testing and dream journaling lays a solid foundation for lucid dreaming. Reality testing builds your awareness, while dream journaling enhances your dream recall and helps you identify patterns and dream signs that may lead to lucidity. Remember that developing lucid dreaming skills takes time and practice, so stay consistent and enjoy the journey of exploring your dream world!

Chapter 10: Oneiromancy: Dream Divination

Oneiromancy is defined as the method of prophesizing the future by deciphering dreams. Although the origins of oneiromancy are shrouded in mystery, there are numerous examples from different ancient cultures, alluding to the age-old nature of the practice. This chapter explores how the practice is viewed in various cultures, including its role and significance and how dreams were seen as sacred messages. Despite its name, dream divination isn't only useful for seeing into the future. Dreams (and the spiritual messages they contain) can also act as a channel for receiving spiritual wisdom and guidance. Oneiromancy can be a unique form of communication with your spiritual guides or higher self. Whether you want to improve yourself or begin an empowering spiritual journey, you can find the way to do it safely through oneiromancy.

Oneiromancy across Different Cultures
Ancient Egypt

Ancient Egyptians recorded their dreams on papyrus.
Djehouty, CC BY-SA 4.0 <https://creativecommons.org/licenses/by-sa/4.0>, via Wikimedia Commons: https://commons.wikimedia.org/wiki/File:%C3%84gyptisches_Museum_Kairo_2016-03-29_Papyrus_03.jpg

The interpretation of dreams can vary between a wide range of spiritual beliefs and cultural traditions. In ancient Egypt, oneiromancy was a science rather than a mythical convention. Egyptians recorded their dreams on papyrus as far back as 2000 B.C. They believed that dream experiences carried missives from their deities, and those able to interpret dreams were oracles blessed by the gods. Vivid dreams and dream imagery with particularly significant details were thought to be divine revelations. To improve their ability to decipher those dream messages, ancient Egyptians often induced prophetic dreams. This was called incubation and was performed in sanctuaries where the practitioners slept in special beds to invoke dreams. They believed that being comfortable made it easier for them to obtain divine guidance, healing, and solutions to various issues. One of the oldest examples of oneiric records is the Ramesside dream book, a manuscript from pre-Hellenistic Egypt. It only has a few surviving fragments, but those all testify to the importance of dream interpretation in ancient Egypt. Another excellent example of Egyptian oneiromancy is the stele lying at the base of the Sphinx. It's adorned with an inscription detailing how Thutmose IV was able to rebuild the statute after consulting his dreams. Legend has it his dreams promised that if he restored the Sphinx, he would become a pharaoh, a prophetic message that became true soon after the restoration of the Sphinx.

Besides using them for documenting their daily life and official mandates, Egyptians also recorded dream divination techniques in guidebooks called dream books. These contained thousands of dream experiences, portrayed and interpreted as signs of events the dreamer can expect in waking life. Due to the fast-growing interest in divination in the past couple of decades, archeologists are discovering more and more Egyptian dream books. Alongside offering guidance on oneiromancy, Egyptian dream books also deliver a stepping stone for contemporary psychology research. In some of the tomes, Egyptians categorized dream experiences, along with the emotions they experienced in their lives, illustrating the predictions (and their results) they made through dream divination.

Ancient Greece

In ancient Greece, dream divination had a different function and was likewise recorded in dream books. Famous Greek philosophers like Aristotle and Plato discussed oneiromancy in several published works. However, far fewer dream books survived from ancient Greece than from Egypt. The only complete one is the Oneoritica, the Greco-Roman piece authored by Artemidorus. Artemidorus credits several other authors for serving as an inspiration for his work, which testifies to the widespread interest in the practice at the time. Artemidorus divided dream divination into two categories. One belongs to the theōrēmatikos, the dreams denoting thoughts and emotions from the most transparent part of the soul. The other one is allēgorikos, which asserts that predictive dreams come from an impure soul, which was a theory previously popularized by Plato. Other authors have also featured dream divination in their work. For example, in Homer's Odyssey, dreams about a gate of polished horn serve as a forewarning for emerging issues for mortals. Like Artemidoros, Herodotus also delved deeper into the different natures of dreams, dividing them into non-predictive and predictive (known as onerous in ancient Greece). The name of the latter served as inspiration for the etymology of the word oneiromancy - the modern term for dream divination.

Mesopotamia

The oldest existing records of oneiromancy come from Mesopotamia, dated 3100 B.C. Mesopotamians (in particular

Sumerians) held dream divination in extremely high regard. Even the kings consulted oneiromancers before making critical decisions. For example, the Sumerian king Gudea (ruled 2144-2124 B.C.) is known for restoring the temple of Ningirsu after receiving instructions for this act in his dreams. The Epic of Gilgamesh features the prophetic nature of dreams. The hero, Gilgamesh, foretold his encounter with his soon-to-be friend Enkidu. Enkidu himself receives prophetic dreams about several of his and Gilgamesh's adventures, including their encounter with the giant Humbaba. Enkidu also learns through his dreams that the gods dictated his impending demise as punishment for killing the Bull of Heaven. He saw this in a vivid dream in which he was grabbed and brought down into the home of Erkalla's God (the underworld). As described in the text, he knew that he was in a place where no one could leave, and there was no light or food. Shortly after his dream, Enkidu fell ill and died.

Another famous example of a person predicting their own demise through dreams is King Dumuzid, a great ruler who reigned ancient Mesopotamia before the Flood. The dream predicting Dumuzid's death is far more cryptic than the one depicting Enkidu's. Dumuzid needed the help of his sister (Ĝestin-ana) to decipher the numerous metaphors in his dream. The dream describes waves rising upon Dumuzid, one reed shaking its head at him and two other reeds becoming separated from one another. Trees rose above Dumuzid's head, and the cover of his churn was removed. His sister interpreted it to mean the waves represented enemies in ambush closing in, the single reed as his mother mourning him, the twin reeds as Dumuzid, and his sister who would get separated by his death. Likewise, she said that the tree rising above him meant that the enemies would catch up with him within the wall of his fortress, while the removal of the churn's cover testified about the evil the enemies brought with them.

Atrahasis (the hero of Atrahasis) also received a nighttime omen. His was about a destructive flood he would experience in the near future. The story implies that Atrahasis was an extraordinarily gifted person (even his name means exceedingly wise) who often received missives from the gods. His dream foretelling the flood was also seen as a divine message because before having it, Atrahasis made an offering to the deity Ea, asking for a prophetic dream.

Besides the harbingers of impending doom, dreams also had another role in ancient Mesopotamia. There is evidence that the Mesopotamians used dreams as channels of communication with other worlds. They believed that the person's soul traveled out of their body while sleeping and journeyed to the places the person visited in their sleep and conversed with the beings they saw at these places. For instance, Enkidu's dream about his death partially fits this category, too, as he traveled to the underworld in his dreams.

Ashurnasirpal II (the Assyrian ruler around 883–859 B.C.) was so enthralled by the divinatory of dreams that he erected a temple to Mamu, an Assyrian dream deity. His successor, Ashurbanipal (ruled 668–c. 627 B.C.), was empowered to overcome a challenging military situation by a message he received from the goddess Ishtar in his dreams. Like many other rulers, Ashurbanipal asked Ishtar (his patron deity) before going to sleep for help to defeat the enemy.

Beyond the literature, one of the most notable, well-known oneiric records from ancient Mesopotamia is the Assyrian Dream Book, which is a collection of tablets archeologists found in the library of Ashurbanipal. The clay tablets hold instructions on how to interpret dreams as signs of future events. For instance, one of the notes claimed that if someone dreamt of themselves fleeing a scene/situation/environment repeatedly, they would lose all their earthly possessions.

The Assyrians and the Babylonians divided dreams into two major categories. One was conducive to dreams emanating from the deities, while the other was malicious ones sent by evil entities. In Iškar Zaqīqu, an assortment of dream omens from ancient Mesopotamia, there are detailed explanations of both types of dream experiences, along with the prognosis of what would befall the person having them. According to the text, these observations were made based on previous real-life experiences of people who had both types of dreams. However, there was a wide range of results from both dream types. People who reported having similar dreams all had different results in their waking life. Iškar Zaqīqu describes dreams about various day-to-day situations, from work to family matters to encounters with people, animals, spirits, and deities to grueling journeys.

Sacred Dreams as a Channel for Receiving Guidance, Messages, and Insights

Due to the long history of dream divination being intertwined with spirituality, dreams are often seen as sacred channels for spiritual revelations. These sacred dreams can be used to receive guidance, messages, and insights from higher beings or spiritual entities, as well as being a way for the subconscious mind to access and communicate with higher levels of consciousness or spiritual dimensions. Ancient cultures resorted to different kinds of oneiric (sacred) dreams, including prophetic, healing, wisdom, guidance, revelatory, and vision-enriched dreams. They used the symbols and other parts to accurately interpret the type of dream they experienced and understand their significance.

In the past, different cultures also used *oneirogen* (dream-inducing) plants and practices to invoke dream experiences, improve a person's consciousness during dreaming, and improve dream recall. While some of these methods are now part of history, some practitioners still resort to empowering techniques (usually more intuitive and reflective, like meditation or breathing exercises) to experience communicating with a spirit, deity, or their higher self. In ancient times, if a person described that they felt transported to another time or place, this gave them credibility that they indeed received valuable information from a higher power. Nowadays, it's all about personal empowerment rather than proving credibility.

Like simple dream interpretation, oneiromancy has also become more accessible to people in modern times. With so many resources available, anyone can try their luck at dream divination to better understand their life and actions. This has generated a vast interest in oneiromancy, and more people have started to seek guidance through this practice.

Beyond providing valuable insight into the future, oneiromancy has been a channeling tool for spiritual guidance for centuries. The roots of this practice can be traced back to ancient cultures and religions, where practitioners affirmed that dreams were a reflection of people's innermost thoughts and communications with the soul and all things spiritual. Nowadays, it's known that what enables this connection is the person's intuition or the gateway to the subconscious. The latter is responsible for registering and deciphering messages you might receive from the spiritual world or your higher self.

By honing your ability to identify and interpret spiritual messages, you're raising your chances of receiving valuable information and improving your well-being and life. One of the main ways oneiromancy helps you achieve this is by improving your self-awareness, which facilitates identifying inner discords. It's easy to see why this is one of the main benefits of the practice, according to contemporary dream diviners. It helps you identify your emotions correctly and manage them more efficiently, enabling you to see conflicts between thoughts and feelings you weren't aware of. Part of the reason behind this is the personal nature of the practice because your connection with your intuition is also very personal. As you tap into your intuition to decipher the spiritual messages you receive, you can see re-emerging patterns and symbols that can indicate an issue you need to address promptly.

For instance, losing a precious object may mean that you're afraid of losing control. Working with your intuition also forces you to explore suppressed emotions. It's much easier to work with spiritual messages without buried (but still festering) negative emotions interfering with the process. Using intuition to analyze spiritual insights may also help you recognize involuntary projections and unconscious thoughts. Both are considered the results of an impaired balance in one's spiritual state. By recognizing them and gaining insight into the emotions behind them, you can enhance your ability of spiritual communication.

Moreover, your subconscious mind can reveal thoughts your conscious mind isn't aware of. Through oneiromancy, you can understand these ideas better, as well as how they affect your emotions, actions, and relationships, including the ones you build with your spiritual self and other entities. That said, even though oneiromancy can be a powerful tool for gaining insight into your inner conflicts and emotions, remember that practice is subjective. It's ultimately up to you how you choose to practice this craft and reflect on your dreams and feelings.

Oneirmacy nurtures self-discovery and personal growth through the numerous insights and assistance you gain from various spiritual sources. Spiritual growth is at the base of advancements in all aspects of life, including personal ones. Besides hinting at your deepest fears, desires, and motivations, spiritual messages can teach you about who you are. You can use dream divination to receive advice on how to tap into your motivation to better yourself. Knowing you can tap into spiritual resources can be incredibly empowering. Sometimes, the spiritual messages will act as a mirror, making you confront what you've been trying to repress or hide. It's another way the spirits or your spiritual help might be trying to motivate you to work toward improving yourself so you can work through your issues and obtain a profound sense of inner balance and understanding.

As you start to understand the messages carried by your dreams, you might feel inspired to make changes in your life that align with your innermost values. When you decide on a path that leads to the fulfillment of your desires, you can ask for additional guidance on how to get there safely and overcome any obstacles that might come your way. By helping you identify your strengths and weaknesses, dream divination can be an essential part of your journey toward self-improvement.

Enabling you to explore the hidden significance and symbolism behind your dreams is yet another way oneiromancy leads to self-fulfillment. As you uncover repressed emotions, unresolved conflicts, and areas where you want to grow and evolve, you find out who you are at your core. Empowered by this knowledge, you can take steps toward fulfilling your potential, start to flourish, and enjoy the benefits of this rewarding journey.

Receiving spiritual messages that contribute to growth and development also influences improved mental health and well-being. The practice relies on finding hidden meanings in your subconscious or accessing spiritual connections. By exploring these meanings and relationships, oneiromancy is a window into your inner world, enabling you to identify all your thoughts and emotions, including negative ones.

For example, if you feel anxious or stressed for no reason, you can use your spiritual connection to find the underlying causes. Then, you use the same bonds to find healthy coping mechanisms for these issues. Harnessing the ability to identify and decipher your own feelings can help you regulate them better. Dream divination can even help you sleep better. Using dreamwork for spiritual communication of any kind requires a formidable intention - and the stronger your intent is, the more likely you'll manifest your dream messages. Given that without sleep, your divination rituals wouldn't be successful, focusing on receiving prophetic messages automatically results in better sleep quality. Moreover, resolving traumas by getting advice on healing or overcoming emotional hurdles will increase your chances of getting restful and restorative sleep.

As you use dream divination to tap into spiritual connections, you become better and better at noting your thoughts, feelings, and actions. With some help from the spirits and your higher self, you make more informed, conscious decisions and intentional choices to remain in control of your life. In the same vein, a deeper understanding of personal issues and challenges through guidance via oneiromancy will empower you to find more effective solutions to your issues.

By practicing dream divination, you can improve many aspects of your life, leading to a more fulfilling and meaningful existence. Once again, it's necessary to emphasize that oneiromancy is a highly subjective practice and can differ based on personal traits and experiences and cultural and religious backgrounds. Examples of this can be found in oneiric records from ancient cultures, where in one culture, one dream was seen as the harbinger of deceit, danger, or death, whereas, in another culture, it was a good omen, prophesizing good things to come. Likewise, a dream about a specific situation could signify something beneficial for one dreamer and something negative for another, depending on their subconscious associations.

When practicing dream divination, it's also critical to consider the sentiments (both physical and mental) associated with the dream. A cold sensation during the dream might allude to a vastly different outcome of future events than a warm one. By paying attention to these nuances, you get a better understanding of your dream messages and the reason they're sent your way. You can use this knowledge to invite positive changes into your life and develop a more profound and insightful understanding of yourself.

Conclusion

As you've learned, the meaning behind dreams has always intrigued people. Theories about symbolism have existed for centuries, and in the recent past, the role of dream experiences has been the subject of thorough research. From overnight therapy to preparing you for potentially dangerous situations to healing, your brain can use dream experiences for many useful purposes. After answering the question of why people dream, you've had the chance to explore different types, including prophetic, lucid, recurring, and false awakening dreams, as well as nightmares and night terrors. You've gained insight into the symbolic language of dreams and discovered that besides collective and archetypal meanings, dreams can also have personal significance to every individual interpreter.

Dream symbols can convey complex ideas, emotions, and experiences in a condensed and metaphorical form. Moreover, certain dream settings or scenarios recur across different individuals and cultures and have shared symbolic meanings. These are called dreamscapes, which the relevant chapter taught you how to interpret based on your unique experiences. The subsequent chapter introduced you to common dream themes, like arguments, being chased, falling, drowning, dying/death, teeth falling out, or even visits from deceased loved ones and others. Besides discovering the possible symbolic meanings associated with these themes and their psychological or emotional significance, you've also learned about the significance of the context, emotions, and personal associations surrounding the symbols and themes in dreams when it comes to deciphering them.

Dream interpretation has been used as a therapeutic tool and can be an incredibly helpful self-awareness resource when digging deeper into the subconscious and emotional state. By exploring diverse approaches to dream analysis and interpretation, the relevant chapter sets you on the right track to develop your own toolkit for this exact purpose. To further empower your dream interpretation journey, you were shown how to remember and recall your dreams more efficiently.

Identifying and understanding recurring patterns in dreams can provide valuable insights into the subconscious mind and offer a deeper understanding of one's dreams. Chapter 8 analyzed each type of common pattern (elements, themes, symbols, experiences, etc.) along with sample interpretations for each and offered numerous easy-to-do step-by-step techniques to identify and understand a dream pattern. The penultimate chapter explained the difference between lucid dreams and regular dreams and gave you helpful advice on what to do and what to avoid when interpreting lucid dreams.

Lastly, you were introduced to the age-old art of oneiromancy, including its definition, origins, and role of dreams in ancient divinatory customs and belief systems. You've learned that the practices of oneiromancy vary greatly among different spiritual beliefs and cultural traditions since dream divination has a long history of being intertwined with spirituality. You could use sacred dreams to receive guidance, messages, and insights from higher beings or spiritual entities and your subconscious.

Here's another book by Silvia Hill that you might like

Free Bonus from Silvia Hill available for limited time

Hi Spirituality Lovers!

My name is Silvia Hill, and first off, I want to THANK YOU for reading my book.

Now you have a chance to join my exclusive spirituality email list so you can get the ebooks below for free as well as the potential to get more spirituality ebooks for free! Simply click the link below to join.

P.S. Remember that it's 100% free to join the list.

~~$27~~ FREE BONUSES

- 9 Types of Spirit Guides and How to Connect to Them
- How to Develop Your Intuition: 7 Secrets for Psychic Development and Tarot Reading
- Tarot Reading Secrets for Love, Career, and General Messages

Access your free bonuses here
https://livetolearn.lpages.co/dream-symbols-and-interpretation-paperback/

References

(N.d.). Science.org. https://www.science.org/content/article/new-algorithm-can-find-hidden-patterns-your-dreams

11 famous lucid dreamers and their stories (#4 is surprising). (2016, November 11). Lucid Dreaming And Dream Meanings By HowToLucid. https://howtolucid.com/famous-lucid-dreamers/

6 steps to help you remember your dreams. (n.d.). Psychology Today. https://www.psychologytoday.com/us/blog/sleep-newzzz/201907/6-steps-help-you-remember-your-dreams

8 reasons you can't remember your dreams, according to experts. (2020, August 20). Mindbodygreen. https://www.mindbodygreen.com/articles/why-you-cant-remember-your-dreams-and-what-to-do

About: Oneiromancy. (n.d.). DBpedia. http://dbpedia.org/resource/Oneiromancy

An Egyptian Science and Its Codification: Oneiromancy from the New Kingdom to Late Antiquity. (2017, December 14). University of Liverpool Events; University of Liverpool. https://www.liverpool.ac.uk/events/event/?eventid=86880

Apsara. (2022, March 26). Emotions in dreams – what do they symbolize? Symbol Sage. https://symbolsage.com/emotions-in-dreams-meaning/

Ausler, N. (2022, October 22). What it means when you see numbers in your dreams. YourTango. https://www.yourtango.com/self/spiritual-meaning-numbers-dreams

Bajori, A. (2019, February 27). 7 tips to start remembering your dreams every night. Verv; Verv.com. https://verv.com/7-ways-to-remember-your-dreams-better/

Barber, N. (2022, October 17). What do dreams of numbers mean? The Sleep Matters Club. https://www.dreams.co.uk/sleep-matters-club/what-do-dreams-about-numbers-mean

Barros, Y. (2015, August 4). Our Sangoma explains what these 10 common dreams mean. Life. https://www.news24.com/life/wellness/body/condition-centres/sleep/dreams/our-sangoma-explains-what-these-10-common-dreams-mean-20150804

Booth, J. (2022, December 5). 5 common dreams—and what they mean Forbes. https://www.forbes.com/health/mind/five-common-dream-meanings/

Brain Basics: Understanding Sleep. (n.d.). National Institute of Neurological Disorders and Stroke. https://www.ninds.nih.gov/health-information/public-education/brain-basics/brain-basics-understanding-sleep

Brandon, N. (2022, March 10). Jungian Dream Analysis: Exploring the Unconscious Mind. Dr Nathan Brandon. https://drnathanbrandon.com/jungian-dream-analysis-exploring-the-unconscious-mind/

Budner, S. (2020, March 30). Wegner's theory of dream rebound: The effect of thought suppression. Exploring Your Mind. https://exploringyourmind.com/wegners-theory-of-dream-rebound-the-effect-of-thought-suppression/

Caceres, V., & Wu, C. (n.d.). Why you remember — or forget — your dreams. Everydayhealth.com. https://www.everydayhealth.com/news/why-you-remember-or-forget-your-dreams/

Carper, S. K. (2023, April 14). Lucid dreaming and interpreting spiritual symbols: A guide to exploring your spiritual journey through dreams. Visiting Subconscious. https://visiting-subconscious.com/lucid-dreaming-spiritual-symbols/

Casale, R. (n.d.). 30 common dream symbols and their meanings. World-of-lucid-dreaming.com. https://www.world-of-lucid-dreaming.com/30-common-dream-symbols.html

Chavers, D. (2021, September 23). What does it mean to dream of objects? Dream Interpretation. https://dreaminterpretation.info/what-does-it-mean-to-dream-of-objects/

Coates, P. (Ed.). (1999). Lucid dreams: The films of Krzysztof Kieslowski. Flicks Books.

Danzey, E. (2021, October 21). Mountains in the Bible - important mountains and meaning. Christianity.com. https://www.christianity.com/wiki/bible/why-should-we-pay-attention-to-the-mountains-in-the-bible.html

dhwty. (2020, March 17). Oneiromancy: Dream Predictions in Ancient Mesopotamia. Ancient Origins Reconstructing the Story of Humanity's Past;

Ancient Origins. https://www.ancient-origins.net/history-ancient-traditions/oneiromancy-and-dream-predictions-ancient-mesopotamia-005726

Dream guidance - dream archetypes. (2017, October 30). Triza Schultz. https://trizaschultz.com/dream-archetypes/

Dream incubation instructions. (n.d.). Philosophy Talk. https://www.philosophytalk.org/blog/dream-incubation-instructions

DREAM INTERPRETATION (Historical). (2018, November 28). Psychology Dictionary. https://psychologydictionary.org/dream-interpretation-historical/

DREAM INTERPRETATION (Historical). (2018, November 28). Psychology Dictionary. https://psychologydictionary.org/dream-interpretation-historical/

Dream Moods dream themes: Animals. (n.d.). Dreammoods.com. http://www.dreammoods.com/dreamthemes/animals.htm

Dream Moods dream themes: Feelings & emotions. (n.d.). Dreammoods.com. http://www.dreammoods.com/dreamthemes/feelings-dream-symbols.htm

Dream Symbolism. (n.d.). Encyclopedia.Com. https://www.encyclopedia.com/psychology/dictionaries-thesauruses-pictures-and-press-releases/dream-symbolism

Dreams in Islam. (n.d.). Islamawareness.net. https://www.islamawareness.net/Dreams/dreams2.html

Dreams, J. I. (2018, August 7). Metaphors and symbols in dreams. Journey Into Dreams. https://journeyintodreams.com/metaphors-and-symbols/

Dreams, J. I. (2020, July 16). The meaning of colors: Color symbolism in our dreams. Journey Into Dreams. https://journeyintodreams.com/colors/

Dreams, J. I. (2022, August 12). 12 Dream Interpretation Techniques to Understand Your Dreams. Journey Into Dreams. https://journeyintodreams.com/dream-interpretation-techniques/

Eatough, E. (n.d.). Why do I remember my dreams and how can I recall them better? Betterup.com. https://www.betterup.com/blog/why-do-i-remember-my-dreams

Ellenbogen, J. M., Hu, P. T., Payne, J. D., Titone, D., & Walker, M. P. (2007). Human relational memory requires time and sleep. Proceedings of the National Academy of Sciences of the United States of America, 104(18), 7723–7728. https://doi.org/10.1073/pnas.0700094104

Estrada, J. L. (2023, April 4). How lucid dreaming can help control nightmares. Dream Journey. https://dreamjorney.com/lucid-dreaming-nightmares/

Eternalised. (2020, September 5). Jungian Archetypes: Self, Persona, Shadow, Anima/Animus. Eternalised. https://eternalisedofficial.com/2020/09/05/jungian-archetypes-explained/

Ferguson, S. (2016, May 17). Falling dream meaning and interpretation. Psych Central. https://psychcentral.com/lib/dreaming-of-falling-into-water

Freud's Dream Theory: Why You Dream What You Dream. (n.d.). Flo.Health - #1 Mobile Product for Women's Health. https://flo.health/menstrual-cycle/lifestyle/sleep/freuds-dream-theory

Greeley, J.-A. (n.d.). Water in Native American spirituality. Liquid life: blood of the earth, life of the community. Sacredheart.edu. https://digitalcommons.sacredheart.edu/cgi/viewcontent.cgi?referer=&httpsredir=1&article=1124&context=rel_fac#:~:text=Water%20symbolizes%20the%20origin%20of,agent%20of%20hardship%20and%20death.

Hartmann, E. (1996). OUTLINE FOR A THEORY ON THE NATURE AND FUNCTIONS OF DREAMING. Dreaming, 6,(2, 1996). https://www.asdreams.org/journal/articles/6-2hartmann.htm

Hartmann, E. (2010). The dream always makes new connections: The dream is a creation, not a replay. Sleep Medicine Clinics, 5(2), 241–248. https://doi.org/10.1016/j.jsmc.2010.01.009

History of Dream Interpretation. (n.d.). Oniri.Io. https://www.oniri.io/post/a-bit-of-history-of-dream-interpretation

Hobson, J. A., Hong, C. C. H., and Friston, K. J. (2014). Virtual reality and consciousness inference in dreaming. Frontiers in Psychology. 5, 1133.

Hopkins, P. (1992). The symbology of water in Irish pseudo-history. Proceedings of the Harvard Celtic Colloquium, 12, 80–86. http://www.jstor.org/stable/20557239

Hopler, W. (2021, May 21). Does God still give prophetic dreams? Crosswalk.com. https://www.crosswalk.com/faith/spiritual-life/does-god-still-give-prophetic-dreams.html

How to Analyze a Dream Using Jungian Dream Analysis. (n.d.). Jonahcalinawan.Com. https://jonahcalinawan.com/blog/jungian-dream-analysis/

How to know the difference between normal and prophetic dreams? (n.d.). Quora. https://www.quora.com/How-to-know-the-difference-between-normal-and-prophetic-dreams

Hurd, R. (2009, December 3). The Cognitive Theory of Dreams. Dream Studies Portal | Dream Research, Lucid Dreaming, and Consciousness Studies. https://dreamstudies.org/calvin-hall-cognitive-theory-of-dreaming/

Juin, C. (n.d.). 5 tips on how to remember your dreams. MOONA.

Kendra Cherry, M. (2008, June 4). Why do we dream? Verywell Mind. https://www.verywellmind.com/why-do-we-dream-top-dream-theories-2795931

Kendra Cherry, M. (2009, October 5). Which Jungian archetype are you? Verywell Mind. https://www.verywellmind.com/what-are-jungs-4-major-archetypes-2795439

Kendra Cherry, M. (n.d.). 9 Common Dreams and What They Might Mean. Verywell Mind. https://www.verywellmind.com/understanding-your-dreams-2795935

Kim, T. W., Jeong, J.-H., & Hong, S.-C. (2015). The impact of sleep and circadian disturbance on hormones and metabolism. International Journal of Endocrinology, 2015, 591729. https://doi.org/10.1155/2015/591729

Kirov, R. (2013). REM sleep and dreaming functions beyond reductionism. Behav. Brain Sci. 36, 621–622. doi: 10.1017/S0140525X13001362

Kirov, R., Brand, S., Kolev, V., and Yordanova, J. (2012). The sleeping brain and the neural basis of emotions. Behav. Brain Sci. 35, 155–156. doi: 10.1017/S0140525X11001531

Krans, B. (2013, September 23). Conquer your fears while you sleep. Healthline Media. https://www.healthline.com/health-news/mental-can-you-conquer-your-fears-while-you-sleep-092313

Krstic, Z. (2021, July 19). How to remember your dreams in 5 steps, according to sleep specialists. Good Housekeeping. https://www.goodhousekeeping.com/health/a37040271/how-to-remember-dreams/

Krstic, Z. (2022, April 23). The real reason why you keep having the same dream over and over, according to experts. Good Housekeeping. https://www.goodhousekeeping.com/health/a39789562/recurring-dreams-meaning/

MacDowell, R. (2019, February 28). The Purpose of Dreams. Sleepopolis. https://sleepopolis.com/education/purpose-of-dreams/

Malory, J. (n.d.). Seasons in dreams. Dreaming Life. https://www.dreaming.life/dream-themes/seasons-in-dreams.htm

Marzano, C., Ferrara, M., Mauro, F., Moroni, F., Gorgoni, M., Tempesta, D., et al. (2011). Recalling and forgetting dreams: theta and alpha oscillations during sleep predict subsequent dream recall. J. Neurosci. 31, 6674–6683. doi: 10.1523/JNEUROSCI.0412-11.2011

Nightmare disorder. (2021, June 5). Mayo Clinic. https://www.mayoclinic.org/diseases-conditions/nightmare-disorder/symptoms-causes/syc-20353515

Pacheco, D. (2020, October 30). How to lucid dream | sleep foundation. Sleep Foundation.

Pacheco, D. (2020, October 30). How to lucid dream | sleep foundation. Sleep Foundation.

Pacheco, D. (2022, January 28). False awakening. Sleep Foundation. https://www.sleepfoundation.org/dreams/false-awakening

Parker, D. (2023, June 3). Spiritual Gift Of Dreams And Visions - Understanding! Birds Idea. https://spiritualask.com/spiritual-gift-of-dreams-and-visions/

Patricia, F., & Psychologist, L. (1636750429000). November 2021: Dreams – connecting with your unconscious mind. Linkedin.com. https://www.linkedin.com/pulse/november-2021-dreams-connecting-your-unconscious-mind/

Pauley, R. J. (2017). Lucid Dreams (J. P. Boutilier, Ed.). Createspace Independent Publishing Platform.

Peters, B. (2015, May 30). False awakening and trying to wake up from a dream. Verywell Health. https://www.verywellhealth.com/what-is-a-false-awakening-3014835

Pietrangelo, A. (2020, October 8). Dreams about being chased: Possible interpretations. Healthline. https://www.healthline.com/health/dreams-about-being-chased

Pietrangelo, A. (2021, January 14). Hair falling out dreams: Possible interpretations & significance. Healthline. https://www.healthline.com/health/hair-falling-out-dream

Revonsuo, A., Tuominen, J., and Valli, K. (2015). "The Avatars in the Machine - Dreaming as a Simulation of Social Reality," in Open MIND, eds. T. Metzinger and J. M. Windt (Frankfurt am Main: MIND Group).

Reynolds, T. (2011, January 26). Meaning of colors in dreams. LoveToKnow; LoveToKnow Health & Wellness. https://www.lovetoknowhealth.com/well-being/meaning-colors-dream

Robson, D. (2021, November 14). Can lucid dreaming help us understand consciousness? The Guardian. https://www.theguardian.com/science/2021/nov/14/can-lucid-dreaming-help-us-understand-consciousness

Roland, J. (2017, August 22). Why Do We Dream? The Role of Dreams and Nightmares. Healthline. https://www.healthline.com/health/why-do-we-dream

Sageleaf, C. (2019, July 22). Meditation for Dream Interpretation. Intuitive and Spiritual. https://www.intuitiveandspiritual.com/2019/07/meditation-for-dream-interpretation/

Salako, L. (2023, January 25). What do colours in dreams mean? The Sleep Matters Club. https://www.dreams.co.uk/sleep-matters-club/what-do-colours-in-dreams-mean

Scarpelli, S., Bartolacci, C., D'Atri, A., Gorgoni, M., & De Gennaro, L. (2019). The functional role of dreaming in emotional processes. Frontiers in Psychology, 10, 459. https://doi.org/10.3389/fpsyg.2019.00459

Season dream interpretation - season dream meaning. (n.d.). Dream Interpretation. https://www.dreaminterpret.net/season

Sigmund Freud Dream Theory. (2023, June 13). Simply Psychology. https://www.simplypsychology.org/sigmund-freud-dream-theory.html

Singh, R. (2023, January 11). Unlocking the power of dreams: Discovering the importance of dreams in emotional, psychological, and physical well-being. Times of India Blog. https://timesofindia.indiatimes.com/readersblog/drbstomar/unlocking-the-power-of-dreams-discovering-the-importance-of-dreams-in-emotional-psychological-and-physical-well-being-49094/

Sitbon, J. (2021, January 12). What is a metaphor? Definition and examples. Content-Writing. https://www.wix.com/wordsmatter/blog/2021/01/what-is-a-metaphor/

Sophia. (2017, August 12). Does your subconscious mind control your dreams? The Wisdom Post. https://www.thewisdompost.com/law-of-attraction/subconscious-mind/does-your-subconscious-mind-control-your-dreams/1003

Sophie. (2023, June 29). The Ultimate Guide to Understanding Oneiromancy Dream Meaning.

Spiritual meanings of dogs in dreams (attacking, dying!). (2023, January 26). Spiritual Posts. https://www.spiritualposts.com/spiritual-meaning-of-dogs-in-dream/

Summer, J. (2021, July 20). What do recurring dreams mean? | sleep foundation. Sleep Foundation.

Summer, J., and Singh, A. (2021, July 13). Dreaming about your teeth falling out? Here's what it could mean. Sleep Foundation. https://www.sleepfoundation.org/dreams/dream-interpretation/teeth-falling-out

Suni, E. (2020, October 9). Nightmares: Symptoms, causes, & treatment | sleep foundation. Sleep Foundation.

The Dreamer. (2021, May 9). Dreams about arguing. Dream Dictionary. https://www.dreamdictionary.org/meaning/dreams-about-arguing/

The Editors of Encyclopedia Britannica. (2020). Nun. In Encyclopedia Britannica.

Time in dreams - dream interpretation and meaning of time in dreams. (n.d.). Cafeausoul.com.

Timperley, J. (2023, April 14). What are the best lucid dreaming techniques? BBC. https://www.bbc.com/future/article/20230413-what-are-the-best-lucid-dreaming-techniques

Took, N. (2021, October 6). Dream incubation – can you decide what to dream? The Sleep Matters Club. https://www.dreams.co.uk/sleep-matters-club/dream-incubation

Top 15 proven ways to REMEMBER YOUR DREAMS better tonight. (2014, January 30). Lucid Dreaming And Dream Meanings By HowToLucid; howtolucid. https://howtolucid.com/dream-recall-remembering-dreams/

Turns out, dreams about dogs can be super important: 5 ways to interpret them. (2022, August 19). Mindbodygreen. https://www.mindbodygreen.com/articles/spiritual-meaning-of-dogs-in-dreams

Understanding the metaphors in your dreams. (2018, September 13). Psychology Today. https://www.psychologytoday.com/us/blog/dreaming-in-the-digital-age/201809/understanding-the-metaphors-in-your-dreams

Vallat, R., & Ruby, P. M. (2019). Is it a good idea to cultivate lucid dreaming? Frontiers in Psychology, 10. https://doi.org/10.3389/fpsyg.2019.02585

Voss, U., D'Agostino, A., Kolibius, L., Klimke, A., Scarone, S., & Hobson, J. A. (2018). Insight and dissociation in lucid dreaming and psychosis. Frontiers in Psychology, 9. https://doi.org/10.3389/fpsyg.2018.02164

Walker, M. P., Liston, C., Hobson, J. A., & Stickgold, R. (2002). Cognitive flexibility across the sleep-wake cycle: REM-sleep enhancement of anagram problem solving. Brain Research. Cognitive Brain Research, 14(3), 317–324. https://doi.org/10.1016/s0926-6410(02)00134-9

Wallace, I. (2015, November 26). The symbolism of dreams & how to make sense of them. The Sleep Matters Club. https://www.dreams.co.uk/sleep-matters-club/symbolic-nature-dreams-make-sense

Wamsley, E. J., Tucker, M., Payne, J. D., Benavides, J. A., & Stickgold, R. (2010). Dreaming of a learning task is associated with enhanced sleep-dependent memory consolidation. Current Biology: CB, 20(9), 850–855. https://doi.org/10.1016/j.cub.2010.03.027

Warner, H. B. (2023, April 13). Unlocking the mysteries of dreaming: Common symbols in dreams and their interpretations. Dreamin Sightful. https://dreaminsightful.com/common-symbols-in-dreams/

Warner, H. B. (2023, April 13). Unlocking Your Intuition: Enhancing Psychic Abilities through Your Dream Journal. Dreamin Sightful. https://dreaminsightful.com/dream-journal-intuition-psyche/

Weather dream meaning. (n.d.). Auntyflo.com. https://www.auntyflo.com/dream-dictionary/weather

Why you should remember your dreams. (n.d.). Oniri.Io. https://www.oniri.io/post/why-you-should-remember-your-dreams

Why Your Brain Needs to Dream. (n.d.). Greater Good. https://greatergood.berkeley.edu/article/item/why_your_brain_needs_to_dream

Zhang, W., & Guo, B. (2018). Freud's dream interpretation: A different perspective based on the self-organization theory of dreaming. Frontiers in Psychology, 9, 1553. https://doi.org/10.3389/fpsyg.2018.01553